VGM Opportunities Series

OPPORTUNITIES IN ANIMAL AND PET CARE CAREERS

Revised Edition

Mary Price Lee
Richard S. Lee

VGM Career Books

Library of Congress Cataloging-in-Publication Data

Lee, Mary Price.
   Opportunities in animal and pet care careers / Mary Price Lee, Richard S. Lee.—
Rev. ed.
      p.   cm.—(VGM opportunities series)
   Includes bibliographical references.
   ISBN 0-658-01042-5 (hardcover)
   ISBN 0-658-01043-3 (paperback)
      1. Animal culture—Vocational guidance.   2. Animal specialists—Vocational
guidance. I. Lee, Richard S. (Richard Sandoval), 1927–   II. Title.   III. Series.

SF80 .L44   2001
636'.0023—dc21

                                                                    00-68498

Cover photograph copyright © Photo Disc

Published by VGM Career Books
A division of The McGraw-Hill Companies.
4255 West Touhy Avenue, Lincolnwood (Chicago), Illinois 60712-1975 U.S.A.
Copyright © 2001 by The McGraw-Hill Companies.
Printed in the United States of America
International Standard Book Number: 0-658-01042-5 (hardcover)
                                     0-658-01043-3 (paperback)

1   2   3   4   5   6   7   8   9   0   LB/LB   0   9   8   7   6   5   4   3   2   1

DEDICATION

For Barb and Rick.

To Dorothy again, sixteen years after the first edition. Still a best, best, friend.

To Pearl, dear neighbor and friend.

To M. J., whose pool and umbrella table have seen a good many of our words written through the years.

For Barry and Claudia, close as friends, close in the arts.

And finally, for Carolyn Field, librarian extraordinaire and caring friend.

With love.

CONTENTS

About the Authors . . . . **viii**

Foreword. . . . . **ix**

Acknowledgments . . . . **x**

1. A New Century and a New Look at Animals and Pet Care. **1**

Preventive medicine. Computers and technology in the field. Care and conservation of wildlife. Pets and psychology. An ever-growing field.

2. Animal Care History: From Magic to Medical Expertise, from Exploitation to Protection **4**

Veterinary medicine in ancient times. A time of darkness. Animal care in France. Rural America. Early humane and conservation efforts. The twentieth century—increasing concern for animals. Today.

3. Working with Animals: Aptitude and Attitude Count **12**

Aptitude for animal care careers. Attitude—equally essential. Interlocking of aptitude and attitude.

4. **Volunteering and Apprenticeship—An Answer to Job Market Uncertainties.** 16

   The animal care employment outlook. Getting a job in a highly competitive field. The many ways to volunteer.

5. **From Initial Interest to Full-Fledged Vet: The Route to a D.V.M. Degree** 20

   Junior high and high school. Choosing a college. College curriculum. Choosing a veterinary school. Cost of veterinary school. Your veterinary school experience.

6. **The Many Fields of Veterinary Medicine** 28

   Small animal medicine. Large animal medicine. Veterinarians on the go. Specialization. Public service. Veterinary research in government. Veterinary research in industry and medicine. Military veterinarians. Zoo veterinarians. Holistic veterinarians.

7. **Veterinary Outlook in the New Millennium** 42

   Veterinary medicine and the economy. Promising fields in veterinary medicine. Women and minorities in veterinary medicine. Salary expectations.

8. **Support Careers in the Veterinary Office: Veterinary Technician, Animal Lab Technician, Veterinary Assistant, Animal Hospital Clerk** 47

   The veterinary technician. The animal lab technician. The veterinary assistant. The animal hospital clerk.

9. **Pets *in* Therapy and Pets *as* Therapy.** 53

   Making the pet a pleasant member of the family. Pets for the sick, elderly, and handicapped. Helping pet owners cope with illness and death.

10. Variety and Excitement in Zoo Work.............. **61**

Zoo directors/supervisors. Zoo curators. Zoo habitat designers. Zoo keepers. Internships—a path to zoo work. Aquarium work—animals of the watery deep.

11. Careers in Animal Shelters **70**

Types of animal shelters. Functions of animal shelters. Characteristics needed for animal shelter work. Shelter jobs. A word about pet stores.

12. Soar with the Eagles: Preparing for a Career with Wildlife **80**

Basic career requirements. Education. Wildlife biologist. Rangers. Wildlife conservation officer. Seasonal work, volunteering, and conservation teen clubs. Earth and animal protection clubs: making a difference. Careers in conservation. Communications. Job outlook.

13. Careers with Dogs: From Pampered Pet to Guard Dog.................................. **105**

Combination careers. Educational and physical requirements. Kennel work—the entrée. Dog groomer. Training careers. Dog breeder. Show dog handler.

14. Horse Fever: Careers Working with Horses **124**

Horse breeder. Stable owner and riding instructor. Horse trainer. Horse massager. Life on a dude ranch. Professional riders. Other track careers and blacksmithing. Education.

Appendix A: Veterinary Medical Schools **138**

U.S. schools. Canadian schools.

Bibliography...................................... **147**

ABOUT THE AUTHORS

Mary Price Lee holds a B.A. in English and an M.S. in Education from the University of Pennsylvania. Mrs. Lee is a member of Phi Beta Kappa. She has published, with her husband, numerous newspaper and magazine articles in addition to many nonfiction books for junior high and high school readers. Among the more recently published titles are:

Everything You Need to Know About Natural Disasters, 1996, The Rosen Publishing Group

Careers for Car Buffs & Other Free Wheeling Types, 1997, VGM Career Books

100 Best Careers in Crime Fighting, 1998, Macmillan Publishing Group

Richard S. Lee holds an A.B. in English from the College of William and Mary. He has spent his working life in the creative side of advertising as a copywriter, interviewer/photographer, promotion program coordinator, and currently as a freelance writer.

FOREWORD

Working with animals is an endlessly rewarding experience. It is also an opportunity to find an outlet for your idealism. You can help save species from slow extinction. You can work to help breed those that are endangered. You can prevent suffering, save the distressed, and heal the sick. You can help others train and take care of their pets. This book will show you the breadth of careers in which you can enjoy your love of animals, from veterinary and preventive medicine, through working in zoos or animal shelters, to careers in wildlife conservation and animal training.

In this new century, there are a variety of ways in which you can work with animals. Many ideas are available on on-line sources of information that have only recently become accessible. We hope that *Opportunities in Animal and Pet Care Careers* will help you find the career that's right for you—one that will bring you rewards beyond measure.

The Editors at VGM Career Books

ACKNOWLEDGMENTS

We wish to acknowledge those who contributed to the earlier editions of this book. We find the input of many still valuable for this edition.

Our thanks to Dr. Donald Abt, the Robert Marshak Professor of Aquatic Medicine and Pathobiology, Dr. John Schrader, and Judy Newcomb, all of the University of Pennsylvania's School of Veterinary Medicine for their enthusiasm.

Antoinette Maciolek, Public Relations Assistant, and Millie Perkins, Public Relations Director of the Zoological Society were very helpful to us. We thank them for their assistance.

We appreciate the cooperation of Dolores Jenkins, Office of Public Relations; Dr. Janet Dolin, Assistant Director of Scientific Activities; and Dr. Karl Wise, Director of Information Management, all of the American Veterinary Medical Association, as well as Leane Benson, secretary, and Deborah Binder, Office of Information (AVMA).

Patrick Navarre, Executive Director of the North American Veterinary Technician Association, was prompt and enthusiastic in delivery of needed statistics in this field. Mr. Navarre is a professor at Purdue University's School of Veterinary Medicine. His courses concern the veterinary technician.

For this 2001 edition we appreciate the help of Bill DeRosa, Director of Secondary Education at the Humane Society of the

United States. His interest, prompt response, and genuine desire to have young people become an integral part of the conservation movement is gratifying. Others at the Humane Society of the United States to whom we owe a debt of gratitude include Lori Blake, Administrative Editorial Assistant; Nancy Peterson and John Snyder of the Companion Animals Department; Carol Bauch, Director of Project Management; and David Saks, Human Resources Manager.

Our appreciation to the very colorful Mr. John Walsh, Director of the Society for the Protection of Animals, whose humanitarian efforts are an inspiration to any animal lover.

Prompt and specific information came with great courtesy from Billy Hooper, D.V.M., Executive Director of the Association of American Veterinary Colleges.

Many thanks to Dr. James Dougherty of the Metropolitan Veterinary Association in Valley Forge, Pennsylvania, for clarifying how veterinary specialization is beneficial to both patient and owner.

We were delighted with the enthusiasm of Donna Van Leer, an editor with Purdue University Press, and Margaret Hunt, Managing Editor of the Purdue University Press.

We also feel a great indebtedness to Libby Ross, Associate Director, Veterinary Medical College Application Service. She led us through the labyrinth of VMCA protocol most patiently.

Also a salute to M. J. Fischer whose kindness (and pool!) have lightened many a working hour.

To Dorothy Huber, one of the "dedicatees" of this book in 1983. Almost twenty years later, she is still a very special friend and a fine writer.

Many thanks to Betsy Lancefield, our VGM editor for many years, and Denise Betts, who recently took over the VGM editorial responsibilities. Also, much appreciation to Trudi L. Buri, Deputy Director of the Wissahickon Valley Public Library, a very savvy and devoted librarian who is ever interested in aspiring writers.

More kudos: The Flourtown Swim Club and Borders Book Store of Chestnut Hill, Pennsylvania. I wrote in the Borders Cafe and made friends with two of the very nice managers, Ted and Judy. My affectionate thanks to my typist and editor/friend, Gwyneth MacArthur, and Missy, her pup. Missy stood by watching the endless details that go into making revisions. Finally, to Kristie Karli, School of Veterinary Medicine, North Carolina State University, class of 2001, who is, besides an "A" student, a superb artist and "mother" of piggies Scrapple, Verna, and Sammy. She and her "oink oink" pals are also appreciated by husband Mike.

CHAPTER 1

A NEW CENTURY AND A NEW LOOK AT ANIMALS AND PET CARE

Today animal care career areas have expanded to include almost as many careers as the leopard has spots. Preventive medicine, computer applications, environmental concerns, and many other developments have penetrated the animal care field and enlarged its scope. And in veterinary medicine, employment opportunities will continue to expand in the early 2000s.

PREVENTIVE MEDICINE

According to Dr. Donald Abt, former Associate Dean of the University of Pennsylvania School of Veterinary Medicine, the basis of veterinary medicine has traditionally emphasized preventive care. Doctors in small animal practice and in equine (horse) medicine have always encouraged owners to provide their animals with preventive inoculations and nutritionally balanced diets.

While economic factors are not usually related to the purpose of preventive medicine, Dr. Abt explains that there is one area in which preventive medicine and finances relate. This area concerns the trend in cattle herd programs, the main purpose of which is to increase productivity and raise health levels through preventive medicine. The herd programs provide many jobs in controlling and eliminating the disease mastitis and in keeping detailed records of fertility cycles, calving dates, and immunizations to create model herds and to enhance the breeders' return on their investments.

COMPUTERS AND TECHNOLOGY IN THE FIELD

The computer did not bypass veterinary medicine as it revolutionized the business world. Today, small and large animal practitioners use computers to maintain medical records and financial balance sheets. The most current technological diagnostic systems are used in many large animal hospitals; they help veterinary surgeons and assistants to identify medical problems and often provide references to other sources of information on a given medical subject.

CARE AND CONSERVATION OF WILDLIFE

Veterinarians and other animal health care workers have advocates in the large numbers of people in our country who are aware of the need for wildlife care and conservation. Not long ago only small, special-interest groups expressed concern over birds and animals lost to declining natural habitats or disappearing because of ecological damage. Today, hundreds of thousands of caring citizens are aware that healthy wildlife is both a humane goal and a necessity if the balance of nature is to be preserved. With this support and publicity, workers in animal care have been able to make wildlife preservation and conservation their specialties.

PETS AND PSYCHOLOGY

Another trend is our preoccupation with fitness. These are holistic times, dedicated to the well-being of the whole person. Personal fulfillment, contentment, and a healthy mind are concerns that share attention with top physical condition. These concerns for emotional fitness extend to animal care. Today, there are *pet psychologists* who will treat neurotic animal behaviors.

When pets are not themselves being analyzed, they may be providing comfort as companions to the aged, as anchors to reality for the mentally disturbed, or as an incentive to action for the physically impaired. "Dumb animal" is simply not an accurate appraisal when one witnesses the miracles that can occur between pet and human. *Animal ecologists* (another growing specialty) have discovered that animals have a special sensitivity to the needs and problems of handicapped people, a seemingly obvious idea that only recently has been recognized. The therapeutic value of pets gives an additional meaning to the word "companion" in *companion animal*—the animal care professional's phrase for pets.

AN EVER-GROWING FIELD

The roll call of fields and specialties within animal care continues to grow each year. From *animal ambulance driver* to *pet bereavement counselor,* total animal care is a priority of the new millennium.

This is good news for you. It means more jobs, more choices, and more opportunities to enter this worthy field and create a lifelong career. The popularity of animal care and an increasing realization of its importance have been helped along by the American Veterinary Medical Association, an organization created to inform, promote, and raise compassion in the world of animal medicine.

CHAPTER 2

ANIMAL CARE HISTORY: FROM MAGIC TO MEDICAL EXPERTISE, FROM EXPLOITATION TO PROTECTION

Magic was the earliest form of medical treatment for humans and animals alike. Practitioners called upon the supernatural to cure all their patients! Fortunately, medicine is now based on the scientific method instead of incantations.

VETERINARY MEDICINE IN ANCIENT TIMES

Veterinary medicine is as old as civilization. Early people in the Mediterranean cultures began to domesticate animals and to turn from a hunting to an agricultural society by at least 4,000 B.C. Throughout large parts of Africa and Asia, a veterinary profession developed to tend to animals that had sickened. The Egyptians, Babylonians, and Hindus all combined human and animal medicine in one practice, while the early Greeks contributed the scientific method and taught animal and human anatomy.

The Babylonians are credited with a significant early step in animal medicine—the isolation of sick animals from the herd. Although ailing animals were treated by magic, these early animal doctors passed the isolation technique on to the Hebrews, who in turn passed on the idea to later Western civilizations.

By the beginning of the second century B.C., veterinary practice had taken root in the agrarian society of India where cattle were the most valuable resource. The Hindu religious concept of reincarnation—and with it the sacred status of the cow—was the basis for serious concern about animal care. India continued to develop animal care, establishing veterinary hospitals in the Middle Ages. Even today, there are government-operated *gosadans* (literally "old cow homes") that are a direct outgrowth of these early veterinary hospitals.

The Greeks were the first people to record detailed veterinary history. In 400 B.C., King Alexander of Macedonia created programs of animal study, and the Greek physician Hippocrates recognized the similarities between animal and human physiology as he plunged into the exciting sciences of pathology and anatomy. More than two hundred years later, Galen, a Greek physician working in Rome, dissected horses and noted his anatomical and physiological observations. *The Hippiatrika,* the first detailed veterinary writing, was developed in the Byzantine Empire by Aspyrtus and Vegetius, acknowledged as the true founders of veterinary medicine.

A TIME OF DARKNESS

From the fall of the Roman Empire until the Renaissance, much medical information—human and animal—was lost. However, the horseshoe was invented during this time, and the *farrier* (or shoer of horses) was the nearest thing to a veterinarian. The horse was one of the few animals in this period that was medically studied. In fact, in 1598, a veterinary work, *The Anatomy of the Horse,* was published. It was a detailed study, although crude by today's standards.

Another scholar, the Benedictine Abbess St. Hildegarde, was also at work during this period preparing a study on animals, fish, and birds. She did not draw from earlier studies of any sort, but gathered voluminous information herself.

The Renaissance arrived to waken an intellectually slumbering world, and among its contributions was a revival of interest in medicine. Advances in the control of human and animal diseases were due in large part to the discovery of the circulation of the blood and to the invention of the microscope.

At this time, people were studying animals in different ways. In the late fifteenth century, an early zoo was created on the grounds of the Regent of France, Anne de Beaujeu. This enterprising monarch raised animals in the stately gardens behind the Royal Palace. She also studied the habits of turkeys, an unseemly pastime for a member of royalty!

ANIMAL CARE IN FRANCE

It was not until 1762 that animal care in Europe was organized into a formal tradition. This development was prompted by a devastating cattle plague that demanded a hasty solution. As a result, the first veterinary college, Ecole Nationale Vétérinaire of Lyons, France, was formed. The college attempted to find ways to combat the plague by methods other than quarantine and slaughter.

Fewer than one hundred years later, the French physician and scientist Louis Pasteur discovered microorganisms and established their relationship to diseases in people and other animals. Pasteur's studies encouraged veterinarians to protect animals from communicable diseases.

The doctor's interest extended also to protecting humans from diseases of animal origin, particularly those transmitted through meats and dairy products. The principles of food hygiene that were begun in the nineteenth century owe much to Pasteur's trailblazing research.

RURAL AMERICA

The first stirrings of concern for animal health in America revolved around a directive, *Liberties of Brute Animals.* The Puritans of the Massachusetts Bay Colony wrote the treatise, a voluntary set of rules governing humane animal care.

It was still to be more than two hundred years before any general animal welfare movement would surface in America; yet between 1650 and 1850 there developed the rudiments of veterinary medicine and a gradual separation of the field from human medicine.

People shipping animals to America—early America counted heavily on cattle, swine, and horses from abroad—had their own way of keeping a disease from spreading. The crews of the animal-laden ships were directed to toss any sick animals overboard. Although a heartless process, this practice prevented at least some of the livestock contamination caused by imported stock.

In these formative years of the developing country, wildlife was considered every citizen's property, to be consumed without restriction or governmental control. Commercial demand for leather, fur, feathers, and meat led to wholesale exploitation of wild animals. Domestic cattle succumbed to disease rather than greed as anthrax, pleuropneumonia, and hog cholera became increasingly prevalent.

Two events within a year of each other meant hope for the protection and care of both wildlife and livestock. The Morrill Land Grant Act of 1862, passed by Congress, provided federal land and funds for education in agriculture, the mechanical arts, and veterinary science. A year later, the American Veterinary Medical Association was founded. Its aim was a full-scale attack on the diseases of domestic livestock. Only in more recent years has this organization been able to concentrate on total care for all animals.

In 1884, Congress passed the Hatch Act, landmark legislation that established the Bureau of Animal Industry within the U.S. Department of Agriculture. The bureau regulated the importation of cattle in order to control contagious pleuropneumonia, the most persistent cattle disease, and other livestock illnesses.

EARLY HUMANE AND CONSERVATION EFFORTS

While there was some enlightenment in the field, cruelty to animals and indifference to their plight were still "givens." Many horses were treated as brutally in life as "Black Beauty" was in fiction. At one time in New York City alone, some twenty-five thousand horses, many drawing streetcars, were poorly cared for and overworked. Henry Bergh, a wealthy New York career diplomat, left the diplomatic service to devote his life to curtailing animal cruelty among the hapless streetcar and carriage horses and other creatures. In a ringing speech delivered on February 8, 1886, Bergh declared that "...the blood-red hand of cruelty shall no longer torture dumb animals with impunity." On that day, Bergh established the American Society for the Prevention of Cruelty to Animals (ASPCA).

Bergh also pressed for the enactment of the Animal Welfare Act of 1886 in New York State. Under its terms, any act of animal cruelty was a misdemeanor with specific penalties. It soon became the model for legislation in other states. Only six days after the act was passed, a Brooklyn butcher piled sheep and calves into a cart like so many bags of grain. The butcher was the first of a parade of violators that year to feel the sting of the new animal protection law.

The following year, a national federation of animal welfare agencies was established in an effort to make welfare programs more unified among the growing number of independent agencies. The move was the beginning of a concerted effort to treat all animals like people's best friends.

While humane societies arose to do their part, health education in the animal field also was expanding. More than twenty-two colleges were offering courses in veterinary subjects. The first public veterinary college was founded at Iowa State College. Today there are twenty-seven colleges of veterinary medicine in the United States and four in Canada. Of the early private institutions of veterinary medicine, only the University of Pennsylvania remains.

For twenty years before 1883, Americans were gradually becoming more aware of the finite nature of wildlife. Spurred by the writings of James Audubon, John Muir, Henry Thoreau, and John Burroughs, people were forming conservation organizations. Since these early efforts posed no threat to industry, they were tolerated. (To a degree, this perspective continues today.) But by 1883, fewer than one thousand of America's onetime bison population of sixty million remained; fur-bearing animals were in danger of extinction; and the passenger pigeon was nearly gone—it would disappear forever in 1914. The American Ornithologists Union, founded in 1883, was the first national conservation group; others like the Sierra Club and the New York Zoological Society subsequently were founded. This latter organization was the first dedicated to wildlife conservation as we understand it today.

THE TWENTIETH CENTURY—INCREASING CONCERN FOR ANIMALS

The first half of the twentieth century saw the establishment of state and federal wildlife agencies designed to promote the careful

use of natural resources, including wildlife. During this time, erad-
ication of diseases continued to be the primary goal of veterinary
medicine. Toward mid-century, especially after World War II, veterinarians began a greater degree of interaction with human medical specialists and increased their involvement with control and
protection of the pet population—characteristics of today's veterinary practice and animal medical research.

In the early years of the 1930s, Alfred Leopold, a professional
forester, began to formulate ecological and evolutionary theories.
He recognized the existence of "ecosystems," the interdependence
of human beings, animals, and environment. By mid-decade, Leopold was questioning the validity of prevailing wildlife management concepts that favored certain species. While game animals
received the major share of attention, predatory animals remained
"second-class citizens."

A major spur to the conservation movement was Rachel Car-
son's book *Silent Spring*. In it, the author demonstrated the dan-
gers of current practices such as insecticide use and destruction of
wildlife and its habitat for commercial purposes. The conservation
awareness she generated led to the formation of the Environmental
Protection Agency and the President's Council on Environmental
Quality and promoted the enactment of the Wilderness Act, Endangered Species Act, and National Environmental Policy Act. A
not-so-gentle ripple had grown to a strong current of concern—
and this time, a woman was proving the pen to be mightier than
the sword.

TODAY

There is a growing interrelationship among the many groups
concerned with animal preservation and animal care. The connection between humans and animals long separated in veterinary

medicine has merged as well. Veterinary medicine has taken an increasingly active role in researching the medical uses of atomic energy, in the application of many drugs with common uses for people and animals, in the research efforts of the space program, and in the control and elimination of zoonoses (ailments common to humans and animals). Veterinarians now interact with agricultural specialists as well, in their common concern for food purity as it relates to animal drugs and animal feed pesticides.

In this capsule history, we have not traced the important contributions to animal care made by zoological societies. Zoos have evolved from places of animal confinement to habitats designed for the understanding and the protection of endangered species, and for the education of people in the importance of preserving the balance of nature. Author-zoologists such as Lawrence Durrell actively promote this essential element of animal care through numerous highly readable books and through the protectionist work performed by his Isle of Jersey Zoo off the English coast.

The tremendous growth of the American pet population provides this final historical note: There are more than two thousand animal welfare organizations in the country today, ranging from small local societies for the prevention of cruelty to animals to national groups. The tremendous pet population has also ushered in a broad range of pet care services, from dog grooming salons to operating amphitheaters for animal shows. Many new animal care occupations offer career opportunities today that did not exist even a few years ago. This book will explore some of them.

CHAPTER 3

WORKING WITH ANIMALS:
APTITUDE AND ATTITUDE COUNT

We as a nation have an ongoing love affair with animals. Americans own and care for 48 million dogs, 25 million cats, 23 million birds, 12 million exotic pets, and 340 million fish!

Although many of us enjoy and appreciate animals, often this interest goes beyond that pleasure to considering a career with animals. If so, you'll need to possess two vital attributes: aptitude and attitude.

APTITUDE FOR ANIMAL CARE CAREERS

Among the attributes of aptitude you will need are robust good health—animal care is physically and mentally demanding, far from the glamorous work too often portrayed in the media. Ministering to an ailing horse may be an around-the-clock job. Placing radio transmitters on hibernating black bears to track their later movements will call for wilderness survival skills as well as physical strength and a high degree of courage.

Whether you are rescuing ducks from an oil spill, changing cat cages in a veterinary clinic, or training dogs for the show ring, your aptitude must include an almost inborn affinity for animals: an ability to handle them where others cannot, a knowledge of their habits coupled with a lack of fear of the animals in your care, and a calm competence that animals can sense about you. With these attributes comes an almost instinctive appreciation of an animal's weaknesses coupled with a healthy respect for its strengths and unpredictability.

You may already know how well you get along with animals; but if your aspirations outweigh your experience in this important respect, you should make every effort to see if your love of animals translates into an ability to manage them. This self-testing must go beyond owning and caring for a pet or two. Volunteering in some area of animal care should help you decide whether it is the field for you.

ATTITUDE—EQUALLY ESSENTIAL

With few exceptions, high income does not exist in animal care any more than glamour does. This is among the most giving of careers, in which the desire to be of help to your fellow-creatures (we are all animals!) outweighs considerations of comfort, be they physical or material.

This altruism—of doing good as you see it in an animal context— is a key element in the attitude you need for fulfillment of your career. But it is not the only element. Your emotional attachment to animals must be tempered with professionalism if you are to maintain a healthy balance in your work. The anger you may face at seeing an injury or injustice done to an animal must be tempered with the knowledge of what to do and with the degree of professional objectivity needed to do it. Without this coolness under fire, you cannot function in a helpful way.

Your attitude must be the result of having come to grips with moral and ethical judgments as well as emotions. Although animals have rights, as the Humane Society of the United States has made clear, they are nevertheless viewed as "products" in a society that depends on many of them for food. They also are viewed as necessary elements of biological and human medical research. New drugs and medical devices cannot be approved for human use until their effectiveness has been proven on animal subjects. Animal shelter employees must constantly deal with the hard facts of euthanasia—"good death" is the Greek meaning for the humane disposition of ill or unwanted animals. Veterinarians and their helpers must cope daily with animal illness and death. These are facts of life and they cannot be changed. Your moral convictions cannot be at war with your work if you are to be happy in it. If you can see the necessity of animals as food products, you may find great personal satisfaction in research designed to improve the health of livestock, or in seeing that such animals are raised and handled under humane conditions. This applies equally to supervising laboratory animals—if you believe that their uses in the testing of medical innovations is a necessary part of improving the quality of life for society.

Your attitude, therefore, must agree with the one prevailing in your workplace. Let's say you are the conservation-minded assistant curator of mammals at a zoo. If the zoo is one where animal health is enhanced and endangered species are nurtured, you will be happy in the contribution you make to these goals. If, on the other hand, the zoo for which you work exists primarily for the amusement of visitors rather than for a higher purpose, you would soon become disenchanted with its policies.

INTERLOCKING OF APTITUDE AND ATTITUDE

It's almost self-evident, then, that aptitude and attitude will interrelate in the well-adjusted animal care careerist. Together, they constitute your basic approach to your career.

Much of your aptitude—the ability to relate to animals, physical stamina, ability to learn, and acceptance of less than great financial rewards—will be reinforced by your attitude, which will be positive, cheerful, calm in the face of frustration, and professional in your acceptance of reality. With such an approach, your rewards will be self-esteem and continued pleasure in a lifetime spent with animals.

CHAPTER 4

VOLUNTEERING AND APPRENTICESHIP—AN ANSWER TO JOB MARKET UNCERTAINTIES

THE ANIMAL CARE EMPLOYMENT OUTLOOK

In veterinary medicine, employment opportunities are projected to expand through and beyond the year 2005. Everything favors general job opportunity in the animal care field. Today there is great interest in animal conservation and enlightened animal care. Paralleling this is a trend to return to the land and its creatures. This urban retreat should spell jobs for individuals in animal medicine, in humane care work, in wildlife and range specialties, and in areas of self-employment. (The enthusiastic horsewoman, for instance, may make her living raising thoroughbreds, racing them, stabling horses for others, and giving riding lessons.)

Although positions in the U.S. Fish & Wildlife Service and jobs at the Humane Society of the United States have increased dramatically, positions in some animal care areas are hard to come by. This is because there are more people attracted to the field than there are jobs for them. Some career areas that might be tempting will simply not have many positions to offer.

Throughout this book, chapters on individual animal careers will detail the job market for a particular field, but a few generalizations are possible here. They will illustrate the differences between job expectations and job availabilities. Many laboratory animal clinician positions are available, including working as a veterinary technician, humane society health technician, or in the more rarefied atmosphere of animal research. A profession such as zoology is somewhat less promising. Zoology encompasses a broad area. Among their many duties, zoologists study animals in their natural habitats, collect specimens for laboratory study, and conduct research on animal diseases.

Other good careers include animal conservation and range and park management. Advanced degrees are a tremendous career boost in these areas. But you may have to wait in line as many of these jobs are already filled.

GETTING A JOB IN A HIGHLY COMPETITIVE FIELD

There are many ways to pursue and secure a job in these popular fields of animal care—even the ones that are difficult to enter. Make sure first of all that you have the specialized education needed for your field. Then build on this academic cornerstone with practical experience. Volunteer work, an apprenticeship, and workshops all offer hands-on education.

Guy Hodge, former Director of Data and Information Services of the Humane Society of the United States, believes that on-the-job training gives the prospective animal care worker the edge. You get to know the management—those people who may be able to give you a helping hand later. You also may learn about job openings before they "go public," and be able to declare yourself eligible.

THE MANY WAYS TO VOLUNTEER

The on-the-job training that Guy Hodge so strongly recommends is best achieved by volunteer work. Volunteering comes in many forms: assisting in a pet shop, volunteering for national park work, or just working with animals on your own in some helpful way.

Volunteering in SPCAs, Veterinary Offices, and Zoos

High school students and college students with summers free are often welcome to pitch in at busy SPCAs, community zoos, or veterinary offices. Generally, volunteer work in such places involves necessary but unglamorous chores like cleaning cages and feeding endless corridors of noisy, demanding creatures. But such chores are performed by almost everyone in the animal care field at one time or another. Even managers of local zoos may find themselves doing shovel-duty on a day when a keeper calls in sick. It's good training, then, to learn from the ground up—literally—how to keep animal surroundings clean!

The 4-H Clubs and Future Farmers

The four Hs of the 4-H Clubs stand for Head, Heart, Hands, and Health. Actually, there should be another H, for Helping. Helping for free—or volunteering—is what 4-H Clubs are all about. Children bake the cookies to sell to help an ailing neighbor; adults volunteer to do the carpentry for the 4-H carnival booths.

Ask a sampling of people what 4-H Clubs are all about, and they'll probably say "agriculture." They are right, in part. Farming and raising animals play strong roles in 4-H activities, just as they do in Future Farmers of America chapters. While FFA concentrates on farm crops and farm animals, today's 4-H Club members also may be learning about a whole range of topics from textiles to computers.

Still, the rural image persists in both organizations, along with their involvement with animals. For instance, some 4-H chapters sponsor Seeing Eye Puppy Clubs. Pups are given to 4-H youngsters to raise for a year. These dogs go everywhere with their families—to the store, on trips, and other places where their future blind owners may go. When the year is up, the dog is ready for formal training and placement as a lead dog. (Ask the 4-H Club near you if they have such a program, or others that involve working with animals. There are 4-H Clubs throughout the country and probably one near you.)

CHAPTER 5

FROM INITIAL INTEREST TO FULL-FLEDGED VET: THE ROUTE TO A D.V.M. DEGREE

If you want to be a veterinarian, now is the time to start planning. *Now* is if you're 16, in college, or even a career changer. This chapter will give you the academic lowdown—the courses you'll want to take to be in line for a place in veterinary medicine.

JUNIOR HIGH AND HIGH SCHOOL

Junior high is the time when sciences seem to overtake other subjects on your roster. This is just fine. Take what is offered and you'll find this knowledge becomes the cornerstone of your senior high school science curriculum. High school science courses—biology, mathematics, chemistry, and physics—are essential. Although you may think they are difficult, they are merely a light-hearted introduction to the rigorous science program college pre-vets must face.

Although this chapter is mainly about the necessary academics, there are some other important preparatory steps for a veterinary career. Caring for neighbors' pets, attending local and state animal fairs and school science fairs, joining the local 4-H Club or Future

Farmers (see Chapter 4 for more on this) and visiting a veterinary school open house if you live near one of the schools of veterinary medicine, will all help you in your chosen career. In addition to giving you a taste of your future work, activities such as these will be looked on favorably by the colleges to which you apply.

CHOOSING A COLLEGE

You should take ample time to choose a college that will prepare you for veterinary school. It may be helpful to consider the possibility of attending a college with a veterinary school. Also, some colleges have pre-veterinary programs—usually the colleges with veterinary schools. Your high school counselor will know which ones these are. You will have access to the veterinary school faculty (they sometimes teach undergraduate science courses) and to animal care clubs. The science courses you take as an undergraduate will very likely reflect the philosophy of the veterinary school. But if you cannot attend a college or university with a veterinary school, your chances of entering veterinary school will be diminished little if at all. Your grades, your college's academic standards, your affinity for the field, and your interest in things outside of veterinary medicine will ultimately decide the issue. For example, running a McDonald's proves to admissions officials that you have skills in management, a tool you will ultimately need in whatever practice you decide upon.

Colleges offer you a great opportunity to turn aspirations into accomplishments. In short, study hard. Top grades *do* count because of the tremendous pressure to get into veterinary school. Extracurricular activities begun in your high school years should be continued and expanded: pre-veterinary club work, SPCA work (paid or volunteer), and summer work on a farm or in a veterinary hospital will help increase your chances of admission to veterinary school.

COLLEGE CURRICULUM

In addition to a well-rounded program in communications skills and social sciences, pre-veterinary students should spend a large segment of undergraduate time in the sciences. Zoology, botany, physical chemistry, and physiology coupled with extensive lab periods will provide a concentrated undergraduate experience in the sciences.

Pre-veterinary students generally complete their undergraduate studies and receive their bachelor of science degrees before entering veterinary school for another four-year program. But there are variations on this pattern that you might want to consider. Some colleges connected with veterinary schools offer a bachelor of science degree in pre-veterinary medicine that is awarded after three years of undergraduate work and completion of the first year of veterinary school. For some students this degree may be sufficient for animal care careers that do not need the credentials of the full-fledged D.V.M.

It is very important to get some type of experience with a veterinarian. Some schools of veterinary medicine will not accept you if you have not had hands-on experience. Try to get a summer job in a veterinarian's office. Even if she or he will not pay you, you will have the experience that many veterinary schools demand. It will also acquaint you with the realities of the field—including cleaning cages!

CHOOSING A VETERINARY SCHOOL

Veterinary Medical School Admission Requirements for the United States and Canada is a useful volume that includes descriptions of each veterinary medicine school. For instance, the entry for the University of California gives application information, prerequisites for admission, and method of evaluation for the potential student.

The number of schools offering programs in veterinary medicine has increased over the years to twenty-seven, plus an additional four in Canada. However, only 35 percent of qualified applicants are accepted into veterinary colleges. This disturbingly low percentage may dampen your enthusiasm. Don't let it! If you can prove you're exceptional, there may well be a spot for you. While veterinary schools look for students who are outstanding academically, they also are interested in people who have gained skills through life experiences.

For example, consider Kristie Karli, a third-year veterinary student, School of Veterinary Medicine at North Carolina State University, with a background as an artist. She brings to her school's program a gift for creative problem solving. Veterinarians have to interact with people as well as animals, therefore experience that requires good communication skills is a plus on an application. Although a good science background is important, today's vet schools also have a greater interest in the well-rounded individual than in the single-minded academician.

Applications for most veterinary schools are handled through an organization called the Veterinary Medical College Application Service (VMCAS). Twenty-four of the twenty-seven U.S. schools and two of the Canadian schools make use of this service. The VMCAS simplifies the application process by allowing the prospective student to file only one VMCAS application and one copy of each required document (such as transcripts). These items are duplicated and forwarded to the schools of the applicant's choice. Some of the participating schools request additional information. The names of these schools are provided in the VMCAS booklet. Any supplemental application materials can be obtained from the individual schools. The VMCAS booklet also lists the schools it does not work with, so that any interested student can contact those admissions offices directly. To order the booklet or for more information on the VMCAS, call 1–877–VMCAS–40 or E-mail them at vmcas@aavmc.org.

Students can apply to any veterinary school they choose, and multiple applications increase the chances of acceptance. Geography, however, may present limitations. If you are not a resident of the state in which the school of your choice is located, it will be much harder for you to get in, and will probably be much more expensive as well. Kristie Karli gives this example: "For my class, there were about 200 in-state applicants for about 70 spaces, and 12,000 out-of-state applicants competing for 12 out-of-state openings. Plus, it costs me about $5,000 a year to go to school, but an out-of-state person pays closer to $20,000 a year. A lot of people move into the state where their top-choice school is located, establish residency (which takes a year in many states), and then apply as a resident. It definitely improves your chances."

States that have no veterinary school of their own will sometimes "contract" with a school in a neighboring state. This allows residents of a state without a school to be considered as in-state students at the school with which their home state has contracted. The student then pays the reduced in-state tuition while, in most cases, their home state also contributes funds to the school. As a condition of this, a few of the schools that have contracts require that those students benefiting from them commit to practicing in the school's state for a given amount of time following graduation.

COST OF VETERINARY SCHOOL

Specific questions concerning pre-veterinary requirements, the cost of education, and the availability of financial aid should be directed to the college or colleges of your choice. And if you wish a compilation of admissions requirements and tuitions for all of the veterinary colleges, write to:

Veterinary Medicine School Admission
  Requirements for the United States and Canada
  Purdue Publishing Co., Inc.
  1532 South Campus Court East
  West Lafayette, IN 47907-1532

Veterinary school tuitions continue to be high. They have increased more rapidly than the costs of other products and services. Today, tuition and fees range from $4,000 to $23,000 per year for residents and $15,000 to $30,000 per year for nonresidents. On the other hand, scholarship aid in the last ten years has held its own. Government loans are available as well as other loan and grant money. Ask your high school or college counselor to guide you to these financial aids.

It doesn't take a math whiz to see that the return on your investment will be a long time in coming. A new D.V.M., with thousands of dollars in educational debts, who takes an entry-level job in the field will be paying back loans for quite a few years. If you're beginning in private practice, the amount of your school debt could be at least doubled by your start-up costs.

It would help, of course, if you could meet undergraduate payments and start your career free of debt. But, you do not go into veterinary medicine solely for the money. It is a profession that attracts a specific kind of person for a most unusual field. That is not to say that ultimately it cannot prove financially rewarding.

Dr. Robert Marshak, former Dean of the School of Veterinary Medicine of the University of Pennsylvania, defends the high costs. Medical school clinics, he explains, enjoy revenues from patients and reimbursement from health insurers. Veterinary medicine has no such remuneration. Dr. Marshak further explains that veterinary medicine is more complex and thus more costly. This is because it deals with different species. Human medicine does not confront animals who differ in the number of stomachs they may have (the cow, for instance, has four stomach-like compartments). Such variations require different kinds of equipment, a greater diagnostic ability, and even different kinds of hospitals.

YOUR VETERINARY SCHOOL EXPERIENCE

Assuming you're accepted and confident that you can make it financially, what is in store for you in your four years? For most veterinary students, graduate school is an exhausting, exhilarating time that can only be eclipsed by work in the actual field itself. It is not for the student who has difficulty with academic work. Veterinary school is extremely difficult and should not be considered unless you are a high-achieving student (other animal fields are less demanding academically).

Kristie Karli has this to say about her academic experience: "The first two years of vet school were difficult due to the tremendous volume of material to be learned (thousands of pages!) but exciting at the same time. For the first time, I drew blood from a giant sea turtle, catheterized a dog, castrated a piglet, spayed a kitten, docked a lamb's tail, dehorned a goat—the list goes on! The third year of studies is a bit more difficult because classes last all day, not including study time, and students start to tire and burn out. There's not as much time to do the 'fun stuff' as there used to be, and the work is more applied, not as new and exciting anymore. The first semester of junior year has been the toughest for me, but I suspect the worst is over. After only one more semester of classroom studies, I will be turned loose in senior clinics to work with real, live animals. It's unnerving, but I can't wait! I'll be seeing my first patient in less than six months!"

As Kristie described, the first two years are mostly spent in class as the veterinary student comes to grips with the basic medical sciences. Anatomy, biochemistry, microbiology, physiology, and pharmacology are among the scientific mainstays. Students learn the normal characteristics of the many types of animals as applied to these disciplines and then study the changes that come from disease and injury. This introductory period could aptly be called "Noah's Ark in Sickness and in Health." (For summer experience, get in touch with the U.S. Department of Agriculture. They regularly hire veterinary students during the summer months.)

The final two years offer hands-on experience. Animal clinic work, laboratory periods, and classes in life-work areas such as veterinary law and public health services prepare the veterinary student for the real world of animal medicine. Although they prepare you to be a veterinarian, vet schools also ready you for animal-related careers in industry, government, the military, and zoos. In the next chapter, you will read about these options.

The typical day of a fourth-year student may go like this: clinical work in a college-affiliated veterinary hospital starts the round of activities, beginning as early as 7:30 A.M. Life can be frantic in this post-dawn period as cases are admitted, histories are taken, and blood work is prepared. Later on things may quiet down, but surgery often highlights the afternoon agenda. Evenings may be free (for study, of course), but the student who started at 7:30 A.M. may have night duty as well.

Not all days are equally hectic. Classwork and library research—many students take dogs under their care into the library!—provide the student with more contemplative work. Both the excitement and the scholarly calm add up to a veterinarian in the making. When the four years are over, the hard-working veterinary student becomes a qualified (and equally hard-working) Doctor of Veterinary Medicine.

Those who plan to go into private practice must pass a very difficult examination—something the renowned veterinarian James Herriot did not have to consider in his day. But then today's veterinarian has tools and expertise that Herriot as a youth never dreamed of.

CHAPTER 6

THE MANY FIELDS OF
VETERINARY MEDICINE

Although human medicine can boast of such pioneering procedures as the artificial heart implant, it was veterinarians who *developed* the artifical heart. Veterinarians were also instrumental in the genetic manipulation involved in cloning (particularly of Dolly, the first cloned sheep). Many of today's 56,694 American Veterinary Medical Association members, plus numerous animal doctors who do not belong to the AVMA, are busy finding ways to expand the production of sea creatures so that there will be more food for the world's growing population. They also are working to control animal diseases that endanger the world's food supply.

Your interest in veterinary medicine may not extend to social issues; you may wish simply to devote your working life to small animals or to join a zoo staff as resident veterinarian. But activist or not, you will be entering a highly rewarding field. Veterinary specialties include many work areas. With your D.V.M. degree you can do any of the following:

- run a small animal hospital
- work in a large animal practice
- enter public service, including the Food and Drug Administration (FDA), the U.S. Department of Agriculture (USDA), or the Environmental Protection Agency (EPA)

- perform research
- join the military
- work with zoos
- teach (academia)

An ever-increasing segment of the veterinary profession is found within corporate-run practices, such as the veterinarian offices in PetSmart stores. Such offices may one day affect smaller private practices because these corporations have the money and power to perform veterinary services somewhat less expensively. These are giant, one-stop, pet superstores—very convenient for the busy, working pet owner, since many such stores and their veterinary offices are open evenings and weekends.

SMALL ANIMAL MEDICINE

If a specialty poll were taken of aspiring veterinarians, 75 percent probably would want to operate or work in a small animal hospital. Your decision—to establish your own hospital, join a practice, or form a partnership—will depend primarily on your financial situation.

Small animal medicine usually involves dogs, cats, and other "companion" animals. "Exotics," which include birds, guinea pigs, hamsters, and reptiles, also figure in small animal medicine. The animal treatment center for these pets is as important to the immediate neighborhood as the library or the firehouse, and the astute veterinarian/manager/owner gives excellent care. Pets are often registered in such hospitals under their own names, as "King George," "Lady Gray," "Burt," or "Wags," rather than under their owners' names.

Private practices today adopt many of the sophisticated methods of human medicine. Intensive care units are now an established part of many veterinary hospitals. Here, teams rather than single practitioners may work to cure sick animals. One team member of great importance is the veterinary technician. Part nurse, part lab technician, he or she monitors the animal's progress while offering comfort and skilled care. (See Chapter 8.)

Small animal hospitals can vary from the modest office with or without an ICU to the giant, university-connected animal care center. Here, the veterinarian works in three basic areas. He or she treats, operates, and advises. This variety may make life a circus for the veterinarian—or at least a cat-and-dog (if not a dog-and-pony) show.

Variety is evident, too, in the increasing number of specializations veterinarians may enter. In recent years, more than twenty specialty fields, neurology and cardiology among them, have been added to the animal medicine roster. Such sophisticated treatments as open heart surgery, the implanting of electronic pacemakers, and chemotherapy are all now a part of animal medical care (much of such work is done in animal-specialty hospitals). There are also mobile veterinary practices, dental veterinarians, and doctors trained to treat the skin diseases of cats and dogs.

A Typical Day for the Vet

For several hours a day, the practicing veterinarian may administer shots, treat accident victims, or do physical examinations. During other hours (or at any hour if a real emergency arises), he or she will be in surgery performing a wide range of operations on sick and injured animals. Also, spaying and neutering healthy animals often make up a major portion of the total surgeries performed in a private practice. Because the animals and their needs vary, the veterinarian's days are bound to be different, too.

Consultations are important: The precepts of preventive medicine are a major part of client appointments. Veterinarians tell puppy and kitten owners the best routes to health—a good diet, proper grooming, correct exercise, and necessary vaccinations.

Dr. Robin Truelove, a Bethany, Connecticut, veterinarian, starts her workday by visiting her post-op patients or the pets she has under observation. A puppy may need patching-up after mixing with a muskrat; a diabetic cat might be next. Before the morning is over, this busy vet may have added a cockatoo and a poodle to her roll call of patients.

LARGE ANIMAL MEDICINE

Dr. Truelove, a rural resident, is also a large animal practitioner. (Country veterinarians often combine large and small animal practices.) After fulfilling her morning tasks, she may head for a local farm to treat a cow with a stubborn case of mastitis, then check out a horse's infected hoof.

Large animal medicine is also concerned with herd and flock care. Veterinarians may oversee livestock, their duties including calving (helping cows give birth), vaccinating herds, and charting herd progress. The veterinarian who opts for large animal practice often takes on a whole stable of responsibilities. As he or she travels from farm to farm, this animal doctor must analyze the condition of the farm, such as its cleanliness and modernity; the personality of its owners (often formidable); and the potential of its herds. Large animal practitioners—and these include U.S. Department of Agriculture (USDA) veterinarians who serve as inspectors—need energy and expertise in amounts almost as massive as the herds they oversee.

Pigs, sheep, livestock, and poultry often qualify as "patients" to the extent that their collective diseases or infirmities can mean damage to the herd, financial loss to the farmer or rancher, and potential danger to neighboring herds. Although herd care rather than individual animal treatment is the norm, the medical challenges are important in terms of the veterinarian's professionalism and the owner's livelihood.

Swine veterinarians are among the highest-paid practitioners. They oversee the herd to maintain health so the farmer benefits from the sale of healthy pigs and the pork is safe for humans. The veterinarian will supervise the herd's diet and its vaccinations and/or antibiotic protocols.

Large animal practice includes equine care, which by its nature tends to be individual care rather than herd-oriented. Equine medicine is growing in importance as these valuable animals, including thoroughbred racehorses, receive treatment unavailable just a few years ago. Horse racing, breeding, and performance require expert knowledge, and the skilled equine veterinarian can offer advice in both medical and behavioral areas. Whether bred for profit, pleasure, or both, the horse has become a focal point of the good life, and its tender loving care is a career for many animal doctors.

A variety of specialties can be found within equine medicine. Besides the thoroughbred and the pleasure pony, there is the role of health inspector for a city's mounted police unit or for horses going at auction. There is the racetrack veterinarian, too.

Equine veterinarians are often surgeons, and some have entered the relatively new subspecialty of equine sports medicine. The health and performance of the racehorse is the specialty of Dr. William Moyer, Chief Equine Veterinarian at the University of Pennsylvania School of Veterinary Medicine. Dr. Moyer often deals with injuries resulting from the tremendous bursts of speed demanded of racehorses. He works to overcome trauma with techniques such as rehabilitative exercises and whirlpool baths. (Injuries often can be avoided by maintaining good muscle tone and applying therapeutic bandaging.)

In many instances, racehorses are owned by syndicates; instead of one owner worrying about his or her million-dollar investment, a whole group gets ulcers when the horse develops problems. Equine specialists like Dr. Moyer feel this tension, too. In many cases, his worry is not so much the horse as its "family."

VETERINARIANS ON THE GO

Many veterinarians travel in well-equipped trucks or motor-home-style vans that contain the equipment they need to treat their patients. Mobile vet practices exist for both large and small animals. (Of course, most large animal veterinarians have to be mobile to some degree because their patients are not easy to transport.) Many traveling vets will have completely outfitted vehicles that constitute an entire practice. There will be an exam room, cages, a surgery room, X-ray and film developing equipment, medicines, and more. The whole vet clinic travels to wherever it's needed.

One such D.V.M. is Francis R. Descant of Willow Grove, Pennsylvania. His practice, House Calls, is totally mobile. Even his patient records are on wheels. So he already knew his patient, Missy, a golden retriever, when he was called to help after she had torn one of her nails in a porch decking crack. Dr. Descant's prompt appearance and professional services soon put Missy back on four feet.

SPECIALIZATION

U.S. News and World Report highlighted a trend in veterinary medicine by subtitling an article "If M. D.s specialize, why shouldn't animal docs?" And while it is true that more and more D.V.M.s are specializing, the American Veterinary Medical Association says that the majority of graduates in this field still become small or large animal practitioners. This may be because the more specialized you become, the farther away you are from dealing with animals. Animal toxicology, for instance, may put you into a lab situation where you never see a four-legged pet or deal with its concerned owner. Another form of specialization is pathology, where the veterinarian performs necropsies (the animal version of an autopsy).

But specialization does not have to mean total isolation. Rather, it allows the veterinarian to skip the worming, nail-clipping, and flea problems common to veterinary practice and confront the more serious—often life-threatening—situations that all pets go through at one time or another.

Pet owners who once reluctantly put their animals "down" when it appeared they were suffering and unlikely to get well, now can often look to several more years of pet ownership. On the other hand, this life-extension can effectively empty a pet owner's pocketbook with hundreds, even thousands of dollars of expenses. Fido may have a pacemaker costing $500 to $1,500; cataract surgery for *one* eye may be $600 to $1,200. Specialization and technology can be a mixed blessing.

The Metropolitan Veterinary Associates, a group of animal specialists* located near Philadelphia, Pennsylvania, make any extra sum of money for animal care definitely worthwhile. Their low-key, but high-quality approach to both the diseases of their patients and the concerns of the owners is a far cry from any financial concerns. They care mightily about their patients and their extensive specialization in a specific area justifies their added training and costs. Those who work at Metropolitan are still basically D.V.M.s—they just reflect a greater interest in a particular aspect of an animal's problems. Not all animals seen by D.V.M.s and vet-

---

*All veterinary specialists must be certified for their field.

erinary specialists are ill or injured. For example, often, a diagnosis is needed to decide whether a female purebred can attend an American Kennel Club (AKC) dog show or if she should stay home because puppies are imminent! Ultrasonic scans can determine this—a procedure that was once used exclusively on humans.

Dr. James Dougherty, a specialist in internal medicine and oncology at the Metropolitan Hospital, believes that internists are simply veterinarians with greater diagnostic skills in a particular field. With more sophisticated training and high-tech equipment, they can do a more in-depth analysis of an animal's problems. Thus they can often back up a primary or regular veterinarian who suggests surgery. The second opinion by the internist gives the pet owner peace of mind in confirming his or her own vet's opinion.

Internal medicine is so broad, says Dr. Dougherty, that often what *appears* to be the problem may be totally unrelated to it. For example, a dog he had once examined had a nasal discharge. The animal's tear ducts were the cause of his discomfort. So the pet had an eye problem rather than a nasal problem. Dr. Dougherty recommended the pet to the hospital's ophthalmologist, or eye specialist. It is this pleasure in making sophisticated diagnoses and the rewards of a pet returning to good health that Dr. Dougherty enjoys the most.

Another service that has accompanied the high-tech vet is the emergency clinic. Certainly veterinarians with 9:00 to 5:00 practices are delighted to leave emergency work to someone else (unless it is an animal under their care). And pet owners with middle-of-the-night worries (seizures, etc.) feel more at ease knowing there is such a service available. There is now an emergency residency in many veterinary schools designed for the recently graduated D.V.M. who likes the excitement of the work and enjoys setting work hours on his or her own terms.

On a light note, we examine the fastidious cat who never quite lets you know what's going on in its conniving brain. A couple in Nova Scotia has gone to extremes for that furry friend, the cat. On St. Margaret's Bay in Indian Harbor, a husband-and-wife team run the Pussy Pause Motel. Their brochure emphasizes the conveniences that the "motel" offers: "luxury suites, enclosed patios, timed electronic ventilation, veterinarian on call." You can bet that the vet assigned to this "beat" will do everything for its feline occupants, including a full CAT scan if required!

PUBLIC SERVICE

The U.S. Department of Agriculture and the Public Health Service (both prime employers of veterinarians) are dedicated to achieving and maintaining high standards of cleanliness and care for domestic and imported animals. The Department of Agriculture employs veterinarians to inspect livestock for diseases and to ensure humane conditions for farm animals in transit. The primary goal of the Public Health Service is protection: the protection of animals against diseases, and the protection of humans who depend upon herd animals for food.

Veterinarians in the Department of Agriculture inspect meat and poultry, oversee quarantine procedures for imported animals and birds, and keep a vigilant eye on conditions in zoos, circuses, and pet shops. It's reassuring to know that there is a vast force of animal care professionals who see that animals—whether they are meat-producing, exotic, or companion pets—are protected.

VETERINARY RESEARCH IN GOVERNMENT

Research offers many opportunities to the veterinarian-scientist. The Department of Agriculture and the U.S. Public Health Service have large divisions devoted to animal research. These activities range from developing vaccines for the control of animal ailments to the improvement of medicines to control parasites.

VETERINARY RESEARCH IN INDUSTRY AND MEDICINE

While the federal government conducts certain kinds of research on behalf of animals and their producers, private industry may have different research goals. Although many companies are also looking for protective vaccines and exciting new drugs, others may even involve the veterinarian in ensuring that pets get good nutrition while pleasing their palates. Veterinarian-researchers in one dog food company may study the reaction of test puppies to a new food. With many companies marketing dog food, such canine test kitchens become serious weapons in the competitive battle for share-of-market.

An extremely valuable form of animal research is comparative medicine, where veterinarians and medical doctors join forces. With "firsts" in open-heart surgery, spinal anesthesia, and similar new techniques to its credit, veterinary research is understandably appreciated. Veterinarians and other animal health professionals are also deeply involved in the animal testing of new medical devices and procedures that precedes their approval by the Food and Drug Administration for human use.

A recent medical report that reflects today's advanced thinking in animal genetics (to name just one subspecialty receiving attention) involves the work of a Pennsylvania veterinarian, Dr. Jonas Evans. Dr. Evans removes six- to eight-day-old embryos from the wombs of highly bred, high-quality cows and implants them in the wombs of cows of lesser genetic quality. The result of this amazing and somewhat alarming-sounding procedure is that a dairy herd can be "upgraded" in a few years instead of the twenty or more required with natural breeding. Meat is more tender, milk more abundant. The lower-quality surrogate birth-cow produces a high-bloodline calf—and the genetically superior cow is immediately freed to create another fetus of genetic superiority for implanting. In addition to domestic advantages, there are international implications; nutritionally deprived countries with poorer-quality cows could produce better, more nutritious "products" with such an implant program.

MILITARY VETERINARIANS

Veterinarians who serve in the armed forces may be involved in research, food inspection, animal sanitation, and disease prevention. They may work in American military installations, or serve at U.S. bases overseas. Much of their work parallels the duties of a civilian veterinarian.

For instance, medical examinations of military watchdogs is similar to the work done in a private small animal hospital. But one outstanding difference is that military animal practitioners may have to take helicopters to remote sites to reach their clients.

Joining the military means donning two uniforms: the military dress, and the doctor's whites. Military veterinarians feel a double sense of pride in serving their country and their profession.

ZOO VETERINARIANS

Chapter 10 is devoted to animal care careers centered on the modern zoo. But because many veterinarians opt for zoo careers full-time or serve as zoo consultants, their duties deserve a mention here.

Opportunities in zoos are limited for veterinarians because there are relatively few zoos. This is why many zoo veterinarians are consultants who devote a certain percentage of their practice time to zoo work in exchange for an agreed-upon yearly fee. The few full-time zoo veterinarians are very lucky to be in a specialty that combines the care of exotic animals with the role of animal preservationist and natural conservator.

Most zoo practice qualifies as "large animal" because of the diversity rather than the size of the animals in the veterinarians' care. But size is surely a factor. Witness the recent need of the Philadelphia Zoo's tiger, Monty, for a tooth extraction. Doctors and technicians at the University of Pennsylvania Veterinary Hospital handled the entire procedure, from anesthetizing the three-hundred-pounder to the removal of the abscessed tooth and the supervision of his post-op recovery. Specialists from anesthesiologist to veterinary surgeon were needed to do the job. One doctor commented, "Looking down a tiger's throat when you extract a tooth is awesome. It's still a bit scary, even when you know the tiger is entirely 'out'!"

A typical day for a resident zoo veterinarian (or typical in-zoo activity for the part-time veterinary consultant) may include steps to control a disease unique to an important animal, an operation on a lion, and working with other zoo staffers in planning healthy, attractive new environments for the animals or advising on dietary needs and changes. These tasks are in addition to the regularly scheduled "rounds." Rounds include those times when the veterinarian roams the zoo, observing all the birds, mammals, and other creatures for signs of trouble.

HOLISTIC VETERINARIANS

The millennium brings with it a whole new approach to this exciting medical field. The magazine *Town and Country* has reported that just as humans are supplementing traditional medicine with alternative methods, pet owners are choosing unusual ways to return their animals to good health. In some cases it is sheer desperation that leads pet owners to the holistic vet's door.

Taffy, a thirteen-year-old cocker spaniel, was dying from a lung ailment. Her owner, Beverly Hills schoolteacher Ruth Pilot, was told by her veterinarian that it would be best to put Taffy to sleep. A friend suggested that Mrs. Pilot take Taffy to a holistic veterinarian. Willing to explore alternatives, Mrs. Pilot met with John Limehouse and his wife, Priscilla Taylor, both of whom are holistic vets as well as certified D.V.M.s. The couple prescribed acupuncture. After a few sessions, Taffy's tongue turned pink and healthy and her wheezing stopped. Mrs. Pilot could enjoy a few more years with her aging pet.

The holistic vet is likely to employ homeopathic substances in his or her treatment plan. Tiny doses of plant, animal, and mineral deposits and a nutritional diet have saved animals pronounced incurable.

Many veterinarians use conventional and holistic methods hand in hand. Before traditional surgery, a veterinarian might try Chinese or other herbs to reduce bleeding and recovery time.

The American Veterinary Medical Association has not overwhelmingly endorsed this new approach to animal care. On the other hand, it is not denying that some results have been spectacular.

For more information about holistic approaches to animal health care, contact the American Holistic Veterinary Association at (410) 469-0795.

As you can see, although the majority of veterinary students might logically select small animal practice, there are many fascinating options open to the graduating veterinarian.

Perhaps one of the more unusual options involves the veterinarians at Alameda East Veterinary Hospital in Denver, Colorado, who are movie stars as well as animal doctors. Several times a year, a crew comes in to film *Emergency Vets,* which is watched by

1.6 million viewers a week on the Animal Planet Cable Station. On the show, veterinarians do what veterinarians *always* do—tend to the sick pets brought in by Denver area residents. The *Emergency Vets* website is www.alamedaeast.com.

CHAPTER 7

VETERINARY OUTLOOK IN THE NEW MILLENNIUM

America is such a pet-oriented country that owners consider a veterinarian as almost one of the family. Opportunities in this field are projected to grow steadily through 2005 and beyond. Part of the reason for this growth is that in addition to families with young children, single adults and senior citizens have come to realize the value of a loving pet. Also, unusual pets such as exotic birds, llamas, and ostriches have recently become visitors to the veterinary hospital.

VETERINARY MEDICINE AND THE ECONOMY

Veterinary medicine is commonly acknowledged as a career with great potential. The pet population is increasing, in part because so many people are moving to the suburbs, where it's easier to keep pets. Consequently, small animal clinics will be kept busy. Rural large animal practices will thrive because of greater scientific interest in the raising of livestock and poultry. As a result, there will be a need for more veterinarians.

PROMISING FIELDS IN VETERINARY MEDICINE

Because veterinary medicine is so diversified, there are areas where the employment outlook is particularly promising. D.V.M. graduates who go on to earn degrees in toxicology (the science of poisons and their effects), parasitology (that area of biology dealing with organisms that thrive within living creatures), laboratory animal medicine, and other specialties will find many jobs with corporations, in the public sector, and in veterinary military service. In addition, the veterinary field has expanded to include space medicine, international disease control, and food production.

WOMEN AND MINORITIES IN VETERINARY MEDICINE

Today more than 70 percent of the students in veterinary schools are women. Yet it was not very long ago that a woman in this field was considered an anomaly. High school guidance counselors would discourage female students from pursuing veterinary medicine as a career because of their perceived lack of physical strength and the difficulty of the work.

But as the veterinary schools filled with women who began proving themselves on campus and later in practice, these fears of inadequacy vanished. There remains, however, a disproportionately low number of minority students and practicing veterinarians.

Where do women veterinarians choose to work? Most of them specialize in small animal medicine. A minority opt for a large animal specialty. Some go into single animal areas—they may enjoy cats so much that they go into feline medicine. The career, in general, appeals greatly to female high school students.

SALARY EXPECTATIONS

The salary figures in the following table provided by the American Veterinary Medical Association reflect the latest earnings information for established as well as beginning veterinarians.

PRACTICING U.S. VETERINARIANS

1997 Earnings

*Mean Individual Income
Before Taxes[1]*

Private Clinical Practice

Large animal exclusive	$ 76,360
Large animal predominant	61,087
Mixed animal	59,076
Small animal exclusive	67,562
Small animal predominant	61,856
Equine	76,089
Other	58,512

Public and Corporate Employment

College or university	$ 75,984
Federal government	68,153
State or local government	65,294
Uniformed services	60,097
Industrial	109,941
Other	72,650

FIRST-YEAR EMPLOYMENT AND SALARIES OF 1998
U.S. VETERINARY MEDICAL COLLEGE GRADUATES

	Percent	Mean First-Year Salary
Private Clinical Practice	76.2	*$36,724*
Large animal exclusive	2.1	37,174
Large animal predominant	5.9	37,522
Mixed animal	12.1	35,914
Small animal exclusive	39.8	37,594
Small animal predominant	12.7	36,321
Equine	3.6	29,176
Public or corporate employment	*4.0*	*$36,964*
University	0.6	17,500
Military service	1.3	43,533
Federal government	0.4	*
State/local government	0.0	*
Industry/commercial	0.3	*
Not-for-profit	0.1	*
Other	1.3	34,265
Advanced Study Programs	*19.8*	*$19,153*
Total 1998 U.S. Veterinary Medical College Graduates	2,171	

[1]Excludes an estimated 12 percent return to owner's equity in practice real estate.

*Insufficient numbers to report values

Veterinarians in private practice can expect business overhead and expenses to consume a considerable percentage of their gross income. On the other hand, a thriving practice run by an enthusiastic, conscientious, and businesslike practitioner will provide a comfortable living.

These figures are averages; those for beginners do not consider debt repayment for education. Income figures also may be higher due to increases in the cost of animal health care and in the cost of living in general.

CHAPTER 8

SUPPORT CAREERS IN THE VETERINARY OFFICE: VETERINARY TECHNICIAN, ANIMAL LAB TECHNICIAN, VETERINARY ASSISTANT, ANIMAL HOSPITAL CLERK

The animal hospital has a strong supporting staff for veterinarians and their patients. These health care workers also may be employed in animal shelters, zoos, and other animal care facilities.

THE VETERINARY TECHNICIAN

Animal care technicians work under a variety of names—animal health technician, paraveterinarian, animal technologist, or veterinary technician. Their responsibilities and duties generally coincide, varying only in the degree of responsibility assigned by the veterinarian. Though titles may differ, there is one constant: this field is hot and getting hotter. One reason is that the new multipurpose animal hospitals with their sophisticated, high-tech equipment have a greater need than ever for these skilled workers.

The paraveterinarian or veterinary technician with a bachelor of science (four-year) degree in veterinary technology will do more and earn more than veterinary assistants graduating from a two-year animal technician program with an associate in applied science or equivalent degree. And just like entering a veterinary medicine program, a strong foundation in the sciences is important before attending a veterinary technical school. Some schools accept a high school diploma; others require some college courses.

The position of animal health technician can be a happy compromise for you if for one reason or another you cannot become a veterinarian. Veterinary considerations aside, it is simply a rewarding job in a number of ways. Just think about the many areas in which veterinary technicians may be involved: animal anesthesiology, assistance in surgery, surgical nursing, clinical conferencing, or animal hospital management. Short of diagnosing, prescribing treatment, and performing surgery, these animal care assistants can offer the animal patient the same comprehensive care as the veterinarian.

Veterinary technicians are considered to be indispensable team members in today's ultramodern intensive care units. Part nurse, part technician, they monitor an ill animal while offering it care and affection.

Veterinary technicians also may work in public health organizations, research institutions, and with manufacturers of pharmaceutical products.

Student veterinary technicians graduating from any of the certified institutions in the country have studied microbiology, radiology, animal husbandry, veterinary parasitology, and other courses designed to give them a working knowledge of the veterinary field. While the curriculum sounds somewhat remote from the goal of animal and pet care, there is generally plenty of opportunity during the two-year study period to work with animals.

Here is a typical curriculum for a veterinary technician or animal science technician.*

Core Curriculum	*AVMA Required Areas of Study*
• fundamentals of chemistry	• orientation to the vocation of veterinary technology
• applied mathematics	• ethics and jurisprudence in veterinary medicine
• communication skills	• principles of veterinary anatomy and physiology
• humanities or liberal arts	• anesthetic nursing and monitoring including instrumentation
• biological science	• biochemistry
	• medical terminology
	• veterinary office management
	• animal nutrition and feeding
	• animal care and management
	• animal husbandry, including: restraint, species and breed identification, and sex determination
	• diseases and nursing of companion animals, food production animals, horses, and laboratory animals
	• surgical nursing and assisting including instrumentation
	• necropsy techniques
	• pharmacology for animal technicians
	• radiography using live animal patients
	• comparative animal hematology
	• veterinary urinalysis
	• veterinary parasitology
	• veterinary clinical biochemistries
	• animal microbiology and sanitation
	• clinical experience in veterinary practice
	• humanities
	• computers
	• animal pharmacology
	• introduction to laboratory, zoo, and wildlife medicine

*Provided by the American Veterinary Medical Association.

As a graduating animal technician, you can expect to earn from $11.20 to $17.93 per hour.

THE ANIMAL LAB TECHNICIAN

Of all the animal careers described in this book, animal laboratory technicians are the *least* involved with animals. Their work generally revolves around the prevention and treatment of animal diseases. Thus, test tubes and serums rather than pets or herd animals are their stock in trade.

But there is one role an animal lab technician or technologist may play that involves both experimentation and the animal world. The supervisor of a hospital or pharmaceutical animal laboratory constantly monitors a menagerie of mice, rats, dogs, rabbits, and guinea pigs. Because these animals are there for research purposes, their environments must be carefully controlled and maintained to high standards, and their behavior must be constantly observed.

William Squires, supervisor of the Animal Laboratory of the Children's Hospital of Philadelphia, Pennsylvania, is responsible for the health of his laboratory animals. Each grouping of animals in the laboratory is separated from the others—rabbits from mice, for instance—so that each animal species is kept at its proper temperature and given its correct diet. Handling is also carefully controlled. Squires holds the animals gently but firmly so that the creatures sense that he is not frightened of them. (An animal sensing fear may try to bite the technician.)

A two-year associate degree in applied science has generally been acceptable for this field, but more and more aspiring technicians and technologists have been taking on four years of college. Science courses predominate in either a two- or four-year master's degree curriculum.

Hahnemann University in Philadelphia, Pennsylvania, stands out as the only college or university (at the present time) to offer a master of laboratory animal science program.

The program is designed for those who already have a bachelor's degree in a scientific field. The two-year master's program combines scientific expertise with business managerial skills. Graduates of the program become managers of colonies (a specific grouping of animals such as mice, rabbits, or primates) or animal laboratory facilities (containing many varieties of animals). They ensure that humane care is provided while scientific investigation is performed.

For those with undergraduate or associate degrees, entry-level salaries are in the $17,000 to $18,500 range and can reach $23,000 fairly rapidly. These are union-controlled salaries in the Philadelphia area for animal science personnel. Salary ranges may differ elsewhere.

Those fortunate enough to earn the master's degree in laboratory animal science may expect around $30,000 as a starting salary in an academic setting and $35,000 to $50,000 in industry. It is possible to attain a salary of $60,000 after many years' experience in this field. The job outlook at any level in this field is a healthy one.

THE VETERINARY ASSISTANT

The veterinary assistant feeds, bathes, grooms, and exercises animals. The job outlook for this position is good. According to the 1998–99 *Occupational Outlook Handbook,* a veterinary assistant earned a yearly average of $17,100.

THE ANIMAL HOSPITAL CLERK

The animal hospital clerk or receptionist is a familiar figure to the pet owner. This is the person who gathers up the trembling cat or dog and talks soothingly. Because people view their pets as family members, they expect the best treatment from the minute they carry in their leashed, caged, or boxed animals. That treatment begins at the front desk. The friendliness and competence of the animal hospital clerk are often the deciding factors in a pet owner's choice of a veterinary hospital or office.

Animal hospital clerks do far more than greet owner and pet. They have a multifaceted job that may include record-keeping, billing, phone duty, making appointments, taking inventory, and expanding on the veterinarian's directions for treatment after the office visit—even to following-up by phone to see how the pet is doing.

An animal hospital clerk need not take courses beyond high school to qualify for this position. However, office skills and some knowledge of animals are helpful.

Starting salaries are generally of minimum wage. They do not rise steeply and even with years of experience, one cannot expect to earn a great deal of money. Many animal hospital clerks, however, add veterinary technology to their list of qualifications, and while still performing their duties as clerks, they also work with animal patients. This results in higher pay down the road.

Given the basic skills just outlined, a job as an animal hospital clerk is an excellent beginning for the student who wants to work while gaining further education in animal care or technology.

CHAPTER 9

PETS *IN* THERAPY AND
PETS *AS* THERAPY

Although a dog can be one's best friend, it also can be a first-class nuisance. Barking dogs and yowling cats are not a joy to themselves or to others. Happily, someone is doing something about it. The pet psychologist (often called animal behaviorist) can help companion animals become pleasant members of their families. Therapy or retraining—often for as long as a year—is what it may take to make a pet a "civilized companion."

Conversely, pets are used in therapy to lessen the pain or loneliness of the sick, the handicapped, and the elderly. Social workers and human psychologists are finding that the unconditional love pets can hold for people and their warm, furry presence can qualify them as effective members of the psychological treatment team.

Both these fields—pets in therapy and pets used as a part of therapy—are recognized as fulfilling important needs. Some veterinary schools are ahead of others in introducing these areas into their curricula.

MAKING THE PET A PLEASANT MEMBER
OF THE FAMILY

A barking, destructive, begging creature is not a household pet but a household *pest*. People will often put up with this obnoxious behavior just as they tolerate their own children's bad manners. But such disruption is unnecessary. Psychologists can analyze unacceptable animal behavior and in most cases can rectify it.

The University of Pennsylvania School of Veterinary Medicine initiated the Center for the Interaction of Animals and Society (with funding from the Geraldine R. Dodge Foundation). The center, composed of researchers, veterinarians, animal behaviorists, psychologists, an anthropologist, several social workers, and two psychiatrists, seeks better understanding of the interaction between animals and humans.

One of the animal behaviorists, Dr. Victoria Voith, has chosen to concentrate on the behavior of the aggressive, unsociable pet. One client was an owner afraid to return home at night to her belligerent Doberman pinscher. The cure for the unfriendly Doberman was to show it who was boss. Since the dog had taken on the role of boss, there was a lot of relearning to do. This repatterning consisted of teaching the dog to become dependent upon his owner. His mistress taught the dog to sit or lie down before he was fed or walked. Gradually, the animal got the point, and the proper household balance was restored.

A New York psychologist, Dr. Donald Tortora is coordinator of an animal behavior-therapy clinic in Manhattan. One of the animal psychologist's recent cases involved a problem almost universally shared by dog owners: pets rearrange the furniture when left alone for long periods. Translated, "rearranging" means they break, overturn or nudge chairs, tables, even sofas, from their normal places.

In most cases, dogs misbehave because they are upset or even bored at being left alone. One solution is to have owners go out and return frequently in the first few days of training, so that the animals at home learn that they won't be left alone for long.

Because it is the "psychology" of animals to react to something their owners are doing—in this case, returning home more frequently—they will gradually let up on the destruction. The cause of their loneliness is perceived as being lessened, so they don't have to continue to "act out" on the furniture. Once this behavior modification has taken place, the owners may again leave for increasingly longer periods because the retraining has been successful.

Charlotte Schwartz, an experienced dog trainer and author of *Friend to Friend: Dogs That Help Mankind,* has said that many dogs would be better off and more obedient if they had even small jobs to do. In her experience, the behavior problems of dogs can usually be solved by giving difficult animals a purpose in life.

Many animals—mostly dogs and horses—indeed have a purpose in life: to provide various degrees of therapy and service to humans.

PETS FOR THE SICK, ELDERLY, AND HANDICAPPED

While companion animals may need a man-to-dog talk every so often to correct unattractive habits, they can in turn prove to be of immeasurable help in solving human-based problems.

Consider this: The love and attention of pets is known to help regulate heartbeat, lower blood pressure, and calm the nerves of their owners. People with animals tend to live longer and are sick less frequently. They are less tense because the animals' bids for attention interrupt whatever work- or home-related stress the owners are feeling. If animals can do this for ordinary, healthy people, think what positive effects they could have on the sick, handicapped, or elderly! Although people have recognized the therapeutic effects of their dogs and cats for centuries, they have only recently applied the knowledge in a scientific way. Thus a new animal career is born.

What is so special about a pet? Dogs in particular give unstintingly of their love while expecting nothing in return. They will pour out affection on demand and provide a soothing kind of companionship. Cats, though often more independent, are also comforting, and their furriness and warmth are a source of pleasure.

Eleanor L. Ryder, a former zoologist and a professor at the School of Social Work of the University of Pennsylvania, works closely with the University's School of Veterinary Medicine. Her most recent interest involves pets and the elderly. These are not the senior citizens of retirement communities and nursing homes but those who are living active, independent lives.

Ms. Ryder finds that most elderly owners thrive on the affection of their pets, and they are more alert because of the animals. The social worker is also interested in the types and breeds of pets most suitable for older people.

While Ms. Ryder studies the benefits of pets for the independent elderly, recreational therapists at the Veterans Administration Center in Salem, Virginia, bring companion animals to visit the oldsters who live at this facility. This very special program of animal visitation is a weekly planned project, and the reaction of the residents to the pets is astonishing. Many, initially slumped in wheelchairs, heads nodding, become alert and animated by the arrival of a gaggle of small animals, brought courtesy of the local SPCA.

The pets dissipate loneliness, encourage alertness, and stimulate underused minds. As Ms. Susan Jones, head of the pet-people program, says, "The program gives the staff something to do with patients besides taking their temperatures."

Animals also offer the same special qualities to the sick and handicapped. They can be particularly helpful to the seriously ill child. A touching case of an "extended paw" involved a twelve-year-old English girl and her mongrel pet, Robbie. Doctors credited the improvement of Alison Hart of Bournemouth, England, to the large, friendly dog. Alison, often depressed about her debilitating kidney disease, was coaxed out of her gloom by Robbie's insistent but loving demand for her attention.

So-called "pets" can go far beyond therapeutic companionship for the elderly or disabled. They can be the eyes, ears, and even the arms and legs of those who need them.

The Seeing Eye in Morristown, New Jersey, is the organization that pioneered guide dogs for the blind, but it is now one of many such helping groups across the United States that train dogs for this purpose. Other groups such as Hearing Dogs and Dogs for the Deaf train animals to serve as the ears for the profoundly hearing-impaired. Just as Seeing Eye and other guide dogs help blind people get safely from place to place, specially trained hearing dogs are taught to alert their masters to sounds such as telephones, doorbells, smoke alarms, and oven timers.

A recent, growing trend is the training of "service dogs." These animals help physically handicapped owners by fetching dropped objects, pulling wheelchairs up ramps, forcing open heavy doors, and doing other tasks that allow their owners to achieve independence despite their handicaps.

All these dedicated groups, from The Seeing Eye to Dogs for the Deaf and Canine Companions for Independence, have several things in common. One, they are nonprofit organizations funded largely through contributions. Two, the fees they charge—if any—pay only a tiny fraction of the cost of training the animals. Three, animal training can take months and cost thousands of dollars.

Many of these organizations train dogs on two levels. One involves adapting the animals for their future work by placing them in the care of foster families for as long as eighteen months until they grow mature enough to undergo the long and arduous formal training needed to develop their particular helping skills. (Often, families volunteer as animal foster parents.) The second training level is that employed by the organization before, during, and sometimes after the animal is assigned to its handicapped owner. Such training is thorough, often difficult, but invariably rewarding. It includes training the animal, seeing that the "match" between dog and owner is right for both (this may take a few tries to get the right pairing), training both together for several weeks, and in some cases, following up to see that the bonding process between animal and owner is working as it should. See Chapter 13, "Careers with Dogs," for more details about training opportunities.

Horses, too, serve as therapists for the mentally and physically impaired. When such people, especially children, learn to ride, their self-esteem improves. Some authorities also have found that riding relaxes muscles and improves balance, fine motor skills, and coordination in the handicapped. While most therapeutic riding programs are volunteer-supported, job opportunities exist in the physical therapy area with concentration on horsemanship, and in training horses for therapeutic riding. You will find more information in Chapter 14, "Horse Fever."

HELPING PET OWNERS COPE
WITH ILLNESS AND DEATH

There is yet another guidance area for the pet psychologist or animal social worker. But in this case, the therapy involves the owner rather than the pet.

Psychologists now realize that owners who must consider euthanasia (the merciful putting-to-sleep of very old or hopelessly ill animals), or those who have just had their animals euthanized, are in emotional turmoil. These professionals help ease the suffering of pet owners by acknowledging their pain and loneliness. The healing process begins by helping them to express their grief.

Kathleen Dunn, a staff member of the University of Pennsylvania School of Veterinary Medicine, has a master's degree in social work. She helps people cope with the death of a pet. Ms. Dunn knows that for some, the loss of a beloved animal can trigger abnormal depression—even thoughts of suicide. But for those fortunate enough to talk with her, recovery usually proceeds in a reasonable fashion. Ms. Dunn tells owners referred to her that such depression after a pet's death is normal. She encourages their expressions of grief and responds with compassion. "I understand. Things are quite different for you. You feel anger and pain. But remember all the happy times you had with your pet."

This emotional aid extends beyond the time immediately after the animal's death. Ms. Dunn, as a bereavement counselor, may talk with an owner several times in the first week, and even into the weeks that follow, to see if there is still difficulty in adjusting to the loss.

This veterinary social worker's activities are not limited to "animal bereavement," the formal title for her work. Ms. Dunn also is available to help an owner through the anxious periods of a pet's major illness or operation. If an owner is too distraught to go through hospital formalities when admitting a pet, Ms. Dunn will fill out forms, carry the pet's blanket, and do whatever else she can to make the situation a bit less painful for the owner. She also will explain the testing or operation procedures and to what degree the doctors expect the animal will recover. This helps the owner achieve a more positive frame of mind.

Bereavement counseling is on the rise because the distress brought on by the loss of a pet is being given more serious attention than ever before.

Thus, pets are helpers for humans, and, in turn, they are helped by caring people. This mutual dependence is as it should be, because each has so much to give the other.

CHAPTER 10

VARIETY AND EXCITEMENT IN ZOO WORK

Classified ads may list jobs from A to Z, but "zoo" is rarely among them. Yet, jobs are there, and many of them are avenues to advancement.

What makes up the zoo "family" (animals excluded)? Large zoos have a director, a resident or visiting veterinarian, a habitat designer, curators, and a photographer who may double as director of public relations. The backbone workers, of course, are the zoo keepers. Smaller zoos hire fewer people, and everyone does multiple jobs. Large or small, the zoo staff works hard almost 365 days a year to showcase its residents to the public.

ZOO DIRECTORS/SUPERVISORS

Many zoo directors have come up through the ranks, with their experience as zoo keepers and curators making them ideal candidates for directorships. Or they may come to their jobs because of a degree in zoology, a background in animal management, or because of the letters "D.V.M." after their names. Whatever their field of expertise, zoo directors often have advanced degrees plus experience in business administration, an understanding of animals' natural habitats, and a dedication to animal conservation.

The director has to orchestrate a multitude of different activities of the zoo: animal nutrition, budget concerns, purchase of animals, creation of naturalistic displays, and everything to do with personnel.

In community and county zoos, the director may have similar duties, but could also serve as curator, librarian, or even zoo keeper when the occasion warrants.

Salaries vary widely, depending on the size of the zoo's city or town. The salary figures quoted in this chapter are high and are typical for employees of prosperous and prestigious zoos. Supervisory positions in such environments (and this involves "hands-on" animal involvement) range from $31,000 to $35,000.

ZOO CURATORS

Zoo curators are in charge of the various zoological units. While there may be only one curator in charge of all animals in a small zoo, large zoos have curators who are specialists in one area: birds, mammals, reptiles, and perhaps fish.

Each curator oversees the buildings that house the animals, creating a comfortable environment that also displays each animal to its best advantage. As curators go through their daily routine, they may need to address a hundred challenges, from an unexpected animal ailment to signs of a hoped-for birth. They may supervise the carefully controlled shifting of animals from cages or habitats, finding the best possible site for each animal.

Here's the profile of a curator who is eminently qualified for her position. Chris Shepard, a Californian, is presently curator of birds at the Bronx Zoo in New York. Years of study preceded her entry into the zoo world. Chris received a Ph.D. in ecology and evolutionary biology before she put her academic background to work in her career with birds, her favorite subject. Fortunately for Chris, there was a curator-training program available at the Bronx Zoo. From this internship, she stepped into the role of curator of birds.

Her charges number into the hundreds—all brightly feathered, exotic birds that take over a building several stories tall. Many are there because Chris selected them. When she chooses her species, she considers both compatibility with other birds and breeding potential. Endangered birds, or those with diminishing populations, earn extra attention from Chris; increasing their population is a real challenge.

Curators generally have advanced degrees in zoology or a related area and have had some previous experience in zoo park management or zoo keeping. In a high-paying zoo—a zoo that pays well because it is fortunate to have tremendous community support (other zoos may have such support as well, but the funding often isn't there)—a curator will have an entry salary of $47,500 and can reach the apex of $59,000 per year. Ph.D.s are almost a "given" in this field, but this does not mean that those with master's degrees cannot get a foothold in the many areas that curators work in.

ZOO HABITAT DESIGNERS

An interesting and more humane movement has taken place in the world's zoos within the last twenty years. The creation of realistic landscapes for zoo animals, often called "landscape immersion," makes people visitors to the animals' world, not the reverse, in which animals are caged and people roam. In many landscapes, zoo visitors are often the ones confined to paths and glassed-in areas, while the animals move freely in re-creations of their natural surroundings or habitats.

This movement has many positive elements for zoo visitors and for everyone involved in zoo operation, from curators to veterinarians to keepers. Among the principal and proven advantages is the more natural behavior of the animals, especially when compared to the stress many species must endure in old-fashioned captivity with its cages and proximity to visitors. This natural behavior, in turn, has improved animals' health and has aided breeding efforts in captivity. This breeding preserves many endangered species in zoos and can even help repopulate natural habitats.

These efforts are aided also by worldwide zoo activities such as the International Species Inventory System and Species Survival Plans. Zoos help one another in animal breeding efforts and with the distribution of birds, animals, and reptiles.

Also, by making it possible for visitors to see the animals in surroundings designed to duplicate their native "homes," attention is focused on the need to preserve these natural habitats and save the animal populations from extinction.

The Philadelphia Zoo is America's oldest, but among the historic buildings, great changes have taken place. An area called "African Plains" re-creates Africa's safari land. Here, zebras, giraffes, and many species of birds live as they would in the wild. In "Carnivore Kingdom" jaguars and leopards inhabit an outdoor exhibit through which visitors walk. These are typical of the unique exhibits being built at zoos around the world.

The Philadelphia Zoo also has a state-of-the-art "Primate Reserve." The twenty-five-acre habitat is modeled after a jungle logging camp rather than the traditional zoo preserve. The area considers the comfort of the primates. The floor is rubbery and soft, letting the animals play or wrestle without injury. There are pipes running throughout the primates' playground. The innovative design has the animals as wide-eyed as the public. They love their ropes and scaffoldings and seem happy and at home.

These surroundings encourage the animals to be more mischievous and crafty. They will play games with the zoo keeper, darting toward the glass wall as the keeper, pretending to be scared, turns his back and walks away. (If he could, a particular colubus monkey would play this game all day with primate keeper Scott Barlow.)

We are emphasizing the zoo movement because it has created a greater variety of zoo-related careers. Although they work for specialized architectural and design firms, zoo designers and habitat designers—also known as zoo horticulturists—combine the knowledge of botanists and biologists with the artistic training of the architect and the skills of the mechanical engineer. Many zoo "worlds" cost millions of dollars and combine real landscaping with forests, streams, and rocks built of fiberglass, metal, poured concrete, and other man-made materials (many animal species would soon destroy totally natural landscaping).

Other zoo jobs have come about through the change in the zoo's role from a source of entertainment for visitors, to a caretaker of the world's animal populations. Many of these are not so much "care" jobs as "knowledge" jobs. The individual responsible for an elephant habitat must know these giant creatures and their habits intimately. What do they eat? Where do they like to sleep? In what greenery are they most happy? How can we meet these needs and still make elephants accessible to visitors?

ZOO KEEPERS

Zoo keepers are primarily responsible for the direct care and feeding of the animals in a particular "house." Whether it is the lion, bird, monkey, or reptile house, as a zoo keeper, you would have intimate daily contact with these animal residents. Cages must be cleaned and hosed or swept (the occupants are usually moved to another cage while this is done), and the animals must be given fresh water and their allotment of food.

But zoo animal keepers are far more than housekeepers. They are also nurses—or at least keen observers of their animals' well-being. Should a monkey, crocodile, or kangaroo show signs of illness, the zoo keeper as trained observer reports any symptoms to the veterinarian, the curator, or others responsible for an animal's condition.

A zoo keeper may also be an expert on animal breeding, be familiar with the irregular habits of rare species, and be capable of arranging animal habitats and assisting with exhibit planning and building.

Parenting is another duty of the zoo keeper. Often, animal-infants are raised in a nursery away from the animal-parent. The animal mother may *not* "mother," ignoring or rejecting her offspring as she sees fit. Or the litter may be so large that a small creature might lose out on the mother's love and nourishment. In this case, the keeper becomes surrogate parent, feeding, rocking, or playing with the baby animal.

Later, when the animal is ready, the keeper may reestablish the youngster in the family setting. The keeper does this with a watchful eye—and often, a prayer. Some animals simply do not get a happy reception, and are summarily rejected by parent or siblings.

Animal education (in zoology or animal husbandry) or extensive work with animals are prerequisites for the job of zoo keeper. Although this is the entry-level job in the field, it requires more training than you might expect.

Santa Fe Community College in Gainesville, Florida, is one of only two schools offering an animal technology program leading to an associate degree. It takes eighteen months to complete the program's five semesters. These include general education courses (English, math, and the sciences) and instruction in animal nutrition, breeding, mammal and aquarium culture, aviculture (bird study), and herpiculture (reptile study).

The program is particularly appropriate considering that the role of today's zoo keeper is not simply maintaining animal cleanliness (although there is plenty of that!), but also one that calls for knowledgeable observation of behavior, understanding of nutrition, and awareness of everything involved in the animal environment. Zoo keepers are in the front lines of those pursuing the goal of preserving endangered species and practicing animal conservation.

Students learn the details of animal conservation and rehabilitation. The students learn by working in their own fourteen-acre zoo with a full complement of animal species. In addition to the academics, the instruction is very much hands-on. The work/school day runs from 8:00 A.M. to 5:00 P.M., and students even act as tour guides for the many groups of schoolchildren who visit the zoo. Under these conditions of hard work and steady instruction, students soon learn whether or not they are suited to this career.

Santa Fe graduates are in demand. The school's graduates are quickly hired by major zoos and biological parks. Although some Santa Fe graduates go on to four-year colleges for further education, 80 to 90 percent find zoo jobs right after graduation. Many zoos that hire one Santa Fe graduate will put in a call for more!

Most but not all zoo keepers are union workers, and their salaries depend on the zoo's location, endowment and budget, union or nonunion status, and the zoo keeper's years of experience. The more modest zoo keeper salaries may be held to $8.00 per hour at entry-level with periodic raises. At the other end of the spectrum, the more affluent zoos may pay the beginning or assistant zoo keeper $12.00 an hour and the senior zoo keeper $14.00 an hour— rates that translate to yearly salaries of approximately $25,000 to $29,600, or more.

Those who aspire to zoo keeper careers can join volunteer zoo-training groups. Interaction between future zoo workers and the large and small animal residents gives a person confidence to continue in this unique field.

INTERNSHIPS—A PATH TO ZOO WORK

There is another way to get into zoo work and that is through a zoo internship program. The Philadelphia Zoo has two intern programs for students. One is the Junior Intern Program for junior-high students. The other is a program for college students or college graduates.

The Junior Intern Program introduces young people to zoo curators, veterinarians, and researchers, as well as to the zoo inhabitants themselves. For someone wishing to go into zoo-related work, this is a great opportunity to see all aspects of zoo life.

If you are a college student or college graduate, the internships take place both in the summer and in the fall. Some pay a small salary; others do not. This program is a much more sophisticated version of the junior-high internships. The college students learn exhibit management, zoo administration, and instruction for children who visit the zoo exhibits. They also are assigned to a zoo department, ranging from public relations to video work.

Many zoos offer internships at various levels. Call your nearest zoo (or one in a nearby city you can reach by bus or train) and find out what programs are available. You've heard people say "I can't get work because I haven't had any experience." Well, here's a chance to gain the experience. It could later put you a notch ahead of others seeking zoo work.

AQUARIUM WORK—ANIMALS OF THE WATERY DEEP

Just as there has been a movement to expand and refurbish zoo habitats, large-scale aquariums also are opening up around the nation. The highly successful National Aquarium in Baltimore started this rush of aquarium-building with an emphasis on realism. Another aquarium to open was the New Jersey State Aquarium and Children's Garden in Camden, New Jersey. Other cities with new aquariums (or those to open soon) include: New Orleans, Louisiana; Louisville, Kentucky; Corpus Christi, Texas; and Chattanooga, Tennessee.

These vast new aquariums offer jobs in a very special area of the animal world. It is not a traditional animal field, to be sure, but it has its own unique appeal. Some of you who have had jobs in small aquarium pet shops may be fascinated by the beautiful fish, sea turtles, and other exotic creatures you worked with. Thus, public aquarium work could be exactly the thing you enjoy most.

Aquarium job titles are as unique as the water inhabitants. At the New Jersey Aquarium, the *director of husbandry* tops the career ladder. He or she is the equivalent of animal curator at most zoos, including the Philadelphia Zoo, which is affiliated with the aquarium. Next in line is the *animal collections manager*. This individual is in charge of the *aquarists*. Aquarists feed the fish and other sea animals, clean whale-sized exhibits, report on the health of all the sea creatures, and even dive among these fast-moving inhabitants. The divers actually answer queries from visitors peering into the exhibits. They field the awed questions of children and adults alike via microphone as sharks and other fish cruise casually by.

Both visitors and employees are intrigued by the accessibility of the exhibits at the New Jersey Aquarium and at many of its newer counterparts. Instead of craning one's neck to see the large tanks of fish or other marine exhibits, as had been the tradition, a visitor to the New Jersey Aquarium enjoys the performance from a sunken amphitheater that features an amazing 170,000-gallon harbor seal habitat.

Another mind-blower is a 3-D re-creation of the edge of the Hudson Canyon—a point many miles off the East Coast where the continental shelf ends. Here, the ocean floor drops thousands of feet into an abyss formed over millions of years.

A job as an aquarium worker probably sounds a lot like being paid to have fun. But despite the job's appealing features, those who work at aquariums have the important responsibility of keeping careful track of the health and well-being of their underwater charges.

CHAPTER 11

CAREERS IN ANIMAL SHELTERS

Animal shelters offer excellent job (or volunteer) opportunities for beginners in animal care. With experience, you can advance in job responsibilities. You might also use that experience as a stepping-stone to a different animal care career.

With a high school diploma—or during summer vacations—you can enter animal shelter work with a paid or volunteer job as a kennel worker or adoption clerk. With that diploma and perhaps some relevant college courses you can apply for a job as an *animal control officer* (also called *humane agent*). With a college degree and further on-the-job experience, you can rise through the organization to become an *animal control supervisor, assistant shelter manager, shelter manager, humane education specialist,* or to the top post in the animal shelter, *executive director* (also called *director of animal services*).

To understand why some jobs have two titles, you should know about the two types of animal shelters. And to see how well you might fit into the picture, you need to know the characteristics that all animal shelter workers have in common.

TYPES OF ANIMAL SHELTERS

There are two types of animal shelters. The first type includes shelters that are operated by SPCAs and humane societies, often in cooperation with local government, which assists with funding and law enforcement. There are more than 550 of these shelters and they are run by executive directors and animal workers called humane agents. These shelters depend largely on contributions.

Approximately 2,000 other shelters are supported by their cities and towns. Their leaders are usually called directors of animal services, and their workers are known as animal control officers. Many of these agencies perform their own law enforcement.

FUNCTIONS OF ANIMAL SHELTERS

Both types of shelters cooperate with community law enforcement agencies and with government agencies to perform the following services for their communities:

- enforce local animal control and licensing laws
- investigate complaints of animal cruelty and other irregularities
- issue citations against law breakers and testify in court against them
- control stray, injured, or unwanted animals
- rescue animals
- care for animals in their custody
- find new homes for animals through adoption
- euthanize animals

With all these jobs to be done, there is much work available for the animal shelter employee or volunteer.

CHARACTERISTICS NEEDED
FOR ANIMAL SHELTER WORK

Some people who have selected animal care careers say they have done so because they relate better to animals than to people. The animal shelter worker should be an exception, since a large part of any job from director to adoption clerk involves a high degree of public contact and calls for good public relations and communications skills. Shelter workers must deal positively with the public while dealing kindly with the animals that are their prime responsibility.

Part of this public relations function involves the often difficult task of making people aware of the animal shelter's mission, which is community service. Unfortunately, the old stereotype of the shelter as being merely "the dog pound" still persists. Although enforcing local dog laws is still one duty, what a shelter worker does today goes far beyond that old-fashioned notion.

Positive public relations also is needed to overcome the negative perception of euthanasia, which is unfortunate but necessary in the face of animal abandonment and pet overpopulation.

Much animal shelter work could be heartbreaking for the people doing it. A high proportion of the animals the worker deals with are not suitable for adoption and must be humanely destroyed. Even with a well-publicized adoption program, the number of interested, responsible homes responding are not equal to the number of homes needed. A shelter worker's natural compassion must be tempered with professionalism and a good grasp of reality if they are to serve the community's need for animal control.

Another characteristic necessary for animal shelter work is the willingness to do the job for relatively low pay, particularly in animal shelters funded by public contributions. In many areas, the funds for shelter operation are barely adequate, and pay is proportionately less than it might be for work at similar levels in other animal care areas.

SHELTER JOBS

Jobs for Beginners

The *kennel worker* is one of the most important support positions in the animal shelter. This job can lead to a promotion within the shelter or to a job as *control officer* or *humane agent.* If you think that you would like to work in an animal shelter but you have no experience, a summer of paid work or of volunteering will give you an insider's perspective on things. As a kennel worker, you will care for both sick and well animals in separate areas; feed puppies, dogs, kittens, cats, and other creatures; keep the animals and their cages clean; and perhaps help with adoptions and take care of some administrative details. If you are not a volunteer, you will very likely get paid only close to minimum wage for your efforts, but you'll acquire that all-important experience in animal care that will prove invaluable in any animal care career you select. As a volunteer, especially if you are in college with an animal-related major, you may be able to obtain course credit for your summer internship. Be sure to find out if you can do this before you start your internship.

The *shelter adoption clerk* helps people to select the pet that is right for them or to reclaim their lost animals. He or she also completes the adoption papers, collects the necessary fees, and instructs new owners in basic pet care. This, too, can be either a full-time job or an internship. A pleasing personality; an affinity for animals; basic typing, administrative, and telephone skills; and a high school diploma are the usual requirements for this position. As with a kennel worker, the opportunity for experience or possible advancement should be more important to you than the earnings.

Animal Services Officer/Humane Investigator

Regardless of the title, this is a high-visibility job in the animal shelter world. Animal services officer is the usual title in the city-operated shelter; humane investigator is the title for the same job in a SPCA or humane society facility. This is the person most often in the public eye as it is he or she who arrives when help is needed to rescue a stranded animal and who carries out such unfortunate necessities as serving a cruelty complaint against the negligent owner of a roadside zoo.

This is a job you may be able to get if you're a high school graduate with good communication skills, a positive manner, and the ability to make sound judgments on the spot. A background in basic law enforcement, animal science, ot veterinary technology is helpful but is not necessary. In several states, your proficiency in animal law enforcement has to be legally certified, often as part of your on-the-job training.

Physically, this job calls for skill in animal handling and control (again, part of training), stamina, agility, and strength. Pure strength is not as important as gentleness and persuasiveness, however.

As a new officer, your first training period should include several weeks of instruction in animal law, recognition of animal breeds and behavior, illnesses, injuries, and symptoms of disease. In the next training period, you should learn animal capture and handling techniques for all the situations you'd be likely to encounter. You'd most likely receive training in dealing with the public as well. Training will vary from facility to facility.

After you begin work—often as a partner with an experienced officer—it usually takes some time for you to become reasonably competent. As a beginner, you might be the vehicle driver, assisting and learning from your partner as you make daily rounds.

Your control team may start the day with a list of requests and complaints to be checked out: a barking dog, a roving monkey, a cat in a tree. Other requests may come in via two-way radio: a pig has escaped from an overturned truck on the interstate or a skunk needs to be removed from a suburban garage.

As you rescue, capture, or administer first aid, your team would try to find the owners of domestic animals and might issue a warning or write a citation for any unlicensed animals. Only when animals have been neglected or mistreated are they taken to the shelter.

Animal owners may not always be cooperative. Whenever a pet owner becomes troublesome or a situation gets out of hand—when your one escaped pig turns out to be a squealing herd!—your team would call for shelter or police reinforcements by radio. In any event, an officer's day is seldom dull.

One such spring day was exciting indeed for Janie Gerber, head services officer of the Aspen/Pitkin County (Colorado) Animal Control Department. Responding to a call, she found a kitten marooned on a rock in a river, trapped by rising floodwaters. Janie called for volunteers from the many spectators that had accumulated, formed a human chain, and plunged into the raging water to rescue the kitten. (A rescuer must always be aware of the safety of potential volunteers. Janie's decision was partly hampered by a lack of rescue equipment.) She succeeded and took the kitten to a local veterinarian even before changing out of her soaked clothing.

Janie, an avid outdoorsperson, performs humane rescue work in Colorado's rugged mountains during the winter snows. She has trained her own German shepherd to help.

Janie is also deeply involved in educating people about the humane treatment of animals and is a favored speaker at area service clubs and scout meetings. She believes that the more people know about the needs of animals, the more responsive—and responsible—they will be.

In some areas, you, like Janie, would aid in public relations by speaking on pet care and shelter operation to civic and school groups. You also would make inspection and enforcement calls on pet shops, zoos, animal processing centers, traveling circuses or shows, and riding stables, either at random or in answer to complaints. When rounds are over, you would enter reports on the animals brought in, the citations issued, and the findings of your inspections.

Humane Education Specialist

With additional schooling beyond high school, your chances for an interesting career in shelter work will grow. Among the jobs available are veterinary technician (see Chapter 8) and humane education specialist. Higher education is the key to shelter management positions as well.

The humane education specialist will have a career with moderate growth. If you enter it, be prepared to get a college degree in elementary education first, with a minor in animal science or biology. You also should plan to live in a large city, since most humane education specialists work for larger humane societies, often in connection with an area's public school system.

Your job would be educating the public—especially teachers who work with young children—on the need for humane treatment and respect for animals. Your responsibilities would very likely include conducting audiovisual lectures, field trips, pet care classes, and wildlife preservation courses. You also might be the public relations liaison between your humane society and the community.

The Humane Society of the United States (HSUS) can provide you with more information about a career as a humane education specialist.

Animal Shelter Management Careers

The top management position in the humane society shelter is that of *executive director;* the counterpart in the city-connected facility is the *director of animal services.* In either shelter, the second-in-command is called the *director of operations* or *assistant director.* In smaller facilities, these jobs may be combined.

The director is like the captain of a ship—in charge of every phase of the operation. He or she must have excellent administrative, personnel management, and public relations skills. In a municipal facility, the director formulates the annual budget, in cooperation with a city council or other governing group, and then operates the facility within the budget. The director also may be expected to raise money if the center operates on a contract that does not cover all its expenses.

The director of a humane facility usually works with a board of directors, of which he or she is an unofficial member. The director also shoulders the important job of fund-raiser. In either facility, the director must maintain a harmonious relationship with the public. He or she often accomplishes this by appearing on local radio and TV talk shows and by seeking favorable publicity for the shelter's programs and operations.

Although directors may rise through the ranks—most often promoted from assistant director—they also may have had experience as veterinarians, commercial kennel operators, or animal science specialists. Since directorship openings are relatively rare, an aspiring director must be willing to relocate when and where an opening appears.

In shelters large enough to need them, the director is aided by an *assistant director* or *director of operations,* whose job it is to take charge of all day-to-day activities from supervising employees to maintaining cleanliness standards and purchasing supplies. The careers leading to this position are similar to those leading to the director's position, including advancement from within.

At both of these top management levels, a thorough knowledge of animal health standards, community expectations, and animal law enforcement are required for the job.

Middle management jobs offer salaries higher than those of animal services officers but below those of assistant directors. These jobs can include *animal services officer supervisor* (or *humane investigator supervisor*) and *assistant director of operations.* These jobs are usually earned through promotion or by changing from one animal shelter to another.

A WORD ABOUT PET STORES

Although they may look like a great place to learn the basics of an animal care career, generally pet stores are like most other retail businesses, which are interested in how well a worker can sell its commodities. A background in sales is more likely to get you a job in a pet store than is experience in animal care.

Unfortunately this lack of skill, compassion, or education on the part of the salesperson often results in improper care of animals not only in the store, but with the buyer who has not been given enough information on the proper care of his or her new pet.

Pet stores often purchase their animals from so-called "puppy mills" and "back yard" (i.e., unprofessional) breeders. Suppliers such as these often breed animals (particularly dogs) specifically to meet the public desire for a particular breed, for instance, one popularized by a current movie. Unfortunately, these suppliers are not scrupulous about other breeding concerns, such as overall temperament, or certain genetic predispositions to various health problems. An unhealthy or mentally unsound animal is not always immediately apparent to pet store workers or potential buyers, and unfortunate results can occur.

When an animal is adopted from a shelter, most often the shelter requires that the animal either be spayed or neutered and receive a rabies vaccine before it goes home to its new family. This is not the case in pet stores. If a new owner does not follow through by having a veterinarian perform these services, the results can be uncontrolled breeding (producing offspring that must be adopted, or, unfortunately, euthanized) and a possible community health risk.

Pet stores often set up businesses in malls and other high traffic areas. With appealing window displays, they draw customers in to make an "impulse buy." People buying a pet based on its cute, fuzzy qualities are often disenchanted once they bring it home and realize that they also must train, walk, and clean up after the animals. Many people will decide they don't want this responsibility and will drop the animal off at a shelter or, in some cases, even go so far as to abandon it far from home.

Pet Supply Stores

A different kind of pet store is one that sells items related to pet care, but not the animals themselves. A store such as this does not offer hands-on experience with animals. It does, however, give you invaluable experience in dealing with pet owners.

Animal supply stores sell everything from iguana food to paw mittens. The larger stores generally have well stocked book and periodical sections. Many welcome animal shoppers (on a leash, of course!) and maintain a community bulletin board posting local animal news along with flyers for lost or missing pets.

Some of these stores work cooperatively with local shelters. They have a section of the store set aside (often behind a glass wall) to showcase shelter animals available for adoption. Rather than staffing this area with a paid store employee, a shelter worker or shelter volunteer will staff it. Adoption times are clearly posted, and the requirements for adoption are the same as in the shelter.

These stores will often provide pet care classes, ranging from obedience training to how to brush your dog's teeth. They generally are taught by local professionals rather than store employees.

Working in a pet supply store can be a rewarding career in itself, or it can be valuable training for another pet care career.

CHAPTER 12

SOAR WITH THE EAGLES: PREPARING FOR A CAREER WITH WILDLIFE

The preservation of wildlife is at a crossroads. On the one hand, continuing pressure exerted by conservation groups once more may be advancing environmental causes, which would help improve the job market in this field. On the other hand, the 1992 battle between environmentalists' efforts to protect the spotted owl against logging in Northwestern public lands and the federal government's wishes to permit logging resulted in a controversial compromise: More than one-fourth of the questioned acreage was given over to logging, thus protecting loggers' jobs. The remaining lands—for the present, at least—have been left alone.

Thus, the belief that wild animals and the wilderness are there for our pleasure and are not in and of themselves valuable, still exists—a holdover from the days when most of this country was uncharted wilderness and land, and when animals were ours for the taking. The degree to which this attitude continues is in part political, but not necessarily pervasive in the government-run parks and forests. As national administrations change, the protectionist-versus-exploitation controversy swings with it.

Most animal wildlife careers are government-funded, either by the federal government or by the individual states. While that funding may fluctuate—and job possibilities with it—the basic course is still in the direction established by landmark groups such as the Sierra Club (founded in 1892) and by later arrivals on the conservation scene: that the need to maintain America's open lands and preserve our native wildlife is essential to the country's ecological future. With the slow but steady acceptance of this perspective, career opportunities will continue to expand, as will work with conservation organizations. But be warned—this expansion is neither strong nor immediate.

The new zoo habitats discussed in Chapter 10 are not designed simply to replicate nature at its most awesome. They are also planned to encourage the reproduction of rare species in nearly authentic surroundings. In many cases, zoos exchange animals bred in captivity with other zoos; in other instances, they release these animals into the wild. Rare monkeys with the unlikely name of golden-lion tamarins have been released by Washington's National Zoo, and are surviving in a Brazilian forest, their only native habitat. Some 135 such projects are taking place worldwide. Among some of the American projects are the return to their native habitats of peregrine falcons and red foxes. The Middle Eastern country of Oman is the site of a project to return the Arabian oryx, a rare type of antelope, to its natural state. The costs of all such projects are high, but the alternative is foreseen as extinction of these species. The reward, conservationists say, is well worth the expense.

These zoo creatures belong in this chapter because it is the conservationist and zoo biologist who will follow and keep track of their adventures in their homelands. Although we are concentrating on conservation work in the United States, a conservation technician stationed in Oregon to monitor the spotted owl might find himself or herself accepting an assignment to help re-orient the Arabian oryx to its Middle Eastern home.

Not all species are adversely affected by today's conditions. In one case, rural Chester County, in Pennsylvania, has reported greater numbers of endangered bluebirds than have been seen in several years. More bald eagles have been sighted in adjoining Montgomery County than in recent memory. And there are other encouraging signs among the rarer creatures in the avian world.

A new species of parakeet, the first new member of the parrot family to be found in more than seventy years, was discovered by Robert Ridgely, an ornithologist with Philadelphia's Academy of Natural Sciences. Ridgely's expedition to the jungles of Ecuador was to monitor the spotted rail, a rare bird. Finding the parakeet was an unusual stroke of luck. The name chosen for it was *Pyrrhura Orcesi* (pyrrhura is the Latin name for parrot family members).

Recently, persistent activities on behalf of a fast-disappearing member of the trout family held up the rebuilding of a small but crucial road for the citizens of Jarbridge, Nevada. Jarbridge consists of about thirty residents living in isolation in a rugged mountain canyon. The road is crucial to their getting to the Jarbridge wilderness area, a beloved campground for recreational activities. Their only way of reaching this area, if they cannot have their road, is to drive out of Nevada, into Idaho, and back south into Nevada! And what member of the trout family is holding up the rebuilding of this road? The bull trout, a species that is protected under the Endangered Species Act. Activists will surely continue to cross swords with those who believe that the act is violating their rights to pursue activities for leisure or livelihood.

BASIC CAREER REQUIREMENTS

Wildlife and conservation work calls for strong mathematical and communications skills. Endurance and a duck's ability to shed water are handy, too, because much of the work is done outdoors, often under difficult conditions. Self-reliance is another good trait to have, since counting the tracks of animals that appear in response to an attractive scent—one method of surveying their numbers—may call for many days of observation alone in deep woods.

Workers in national and state parks may be involved in both animal and people management, one place where communications enters the picture. Also, animal technicians who manage wildlife and land resources must be skilled statistical analysts and reporters, able to chart and interpret changes in migration and feeding patterns and animal populations.

Your duties might include the banding of wild animals and birds, conducting wildlife and ecological surveys, animal population regulation, the preservation or development of natural habitats to help in animal propagation, experimentation with bird and animal food sources, and the protection and rescue of animals from natural or man-made disasters.

Other duties include the enforcement of fishing, hunting, and camping laws; park direction; communication; and public relations.

Wildlife technicians work for a variety of agencies including industry, state fish and game commissions, privately funded wildlife preserves, and conservation organizations. The largest single employer, however, is the federal government. Federal jobs—all acquired through Civil Service—are in the National Park Service, U.S. Forest Service, and U.S. Fish and Wildlife Service. Salaries are listed in "GS" categories, the standard applied to all federal careers.

Beginning jobs tend to be the ones most directly associated with animals. Advancement in wildlife and conservation careers more often than not involves increasing amounts of laboratory and research work and administration. It is strange indeed that advancement often means forsaking close contact with animals. At this point, where *up* means *out,* some workers in the animal field will go into a new area just to remain near animal life.

EDUCATION

For all but the most basic work, a bachelor's degree in wildlife biology, ecology, or zoology is essential. Advancement in this field calls for advanced degrees, too. In high school you would concentrate on biology and the natural sciences. College will offer opportunities to specialize further—in wildlife and range management, ecology, forestry (because of its interaction with animals), and other areas. Research methodology is also extremely helpful, tying in with the other study areas.

Seasonal employment and volunteering, discussed later in this chapter, provide on-site education as well as the opportunity to work in the field of your choice before you start college and during summer vacations.

Growing numbers of states require a bachelor's degree for work as forest or park rangers, fish and game control officers, and assistant biologists. As mentioned before, higher degrees are almost essential, particularly if you wish to be a wildlife manager. Students with a B.S. have less than a 50 percent chance of landing a job; master's degree holders may have a near-100 percent hiring record, and Ph.D.'s can almost write their own job tickets. Also, since wildlife management and conservation deal with many state and federal regulations, an understanding of basic criminal justice and of animal laws and their enforcement is part of many jobs. This knowledge can be learned on the job as well as being part of your formal education.

Although veterinary schools often concentrate on domestic animals, a fascinating exception is the Wildlife Service of the University of Pennsylvania's veterinary school. Here, pigeons, gerbils, geese, finches, and other injured or ill animals have been treated by the students. A five-year-old Bengal lizard named Big Red has been a patient. Anyone finding an injured wild bird or animal may bring it in twenty-four hours a day for treatment. There is no charge, but donations are appreciated. In a recent year, the clinic treated 160 wild creatures.

This Wildlife Service is run by the first- and second-year veterinary students. Course credit is given. A term paper is required for full credit and encompasses such topics as how an owl tracks its prey. (Answer: through the auditory system.)

Do the captive, injured creatures take to their helpers? "They're not very appreciative of our efforts," said Jim Reed, one of the participating students. He believes the results are worth the effort, even though the creatures do not show affection or appreciation like domestic pets.

Legally owned exotic animals also are treated at the clinic, for a fee. One visitor, a five-year-old parrot named Tillie, had plucked away her chest feathers from boredom. Her prescription? A change of diet, play toys—and repositioning Tillie's cage by a window and near a turned-on television! Other animals have been treated by every veterinary method from nail-clipping to antibiotics and major surgery.

WILDLIFE BIOLOGIST

The wildlife biologist is the one careerist who is most directly involved with the ongoing safety and well-being of wild animals. A wildlife biologist may spend days in winter camp, as Brad Allen, Randy Cross, and others did northwest of Ashland, Maine. Allen and his teammates were on the trail of fifty hibernating black bears that they had fitted with radio-signaling collars the summer before. The biologists, working for the Maine Department of Inland Fisheries and Wildlife, tracked the bears to see how many had given birth to cubs, how many cubs they had apiece, and how healthy they appeared. The biologists used their data to estimate what the future black bear population would be.

In addition to learning about the habits and characteristics of black bears, their studies helped the state of Maine determine how many bears could—or should—legally be hunted without endangering the species. Since hunting is a multimillion-dollar business in the state, the team's research was important to the economy as well as to the animals.

In answer to an ever-louder "beep" signal, the team moved in on snowshoes to a bear's hibernation spot, usually a ground-hollow or a brush-concealed hole. One team member would cover the opening with a nylon net while another tranquilized the bear with a gun on a pole. Then, they all carefully removed the bear—no easy job at 130 dead-weight pounds—and the cubs. These were kept warm in the biologists' jackets while they were weighed and their ears were tagged for later study. After weighing and recording, all the bears were replaced and the hole re-covered with underbrush to keep the cubs inside. The whole job had to be done in forty-five minutes, the effective tranquilizer time.

The "bear study," as it was informally called, continued for some years. Three teams of biologists worked for three to four weeks in winter and for five months every spring and summer. Winter quarters were primitive—wood-heated cabins twenty-five miles from civilization in the Aroostook County woods. The only access to the outside world was by snowmobile.

If you become a wildlife biologist, you may concentrate in one animal area, or you could work more generally in animal management. In any case, the biologist's work tends to be mission-oriented: basic observation and research aimed at solving or preventing problems related to wild animals and their habitats.

Habitat study is a key. One of the goals is to control the forest habitat to maintain the proper ecological balance of and for different creatures. If forest cutting is to be done, for instance, the wildlife biologist would work with foresters to decide what types of timber to cut, where to cut, and how much to cut. Cutting large stands of mature timber would benefit species seeking new growth for cover or food, but at the expense of hawks, owls, woodpeckers, and other creatures that need older growth.

In a national forest where your work is coordinated with foresters and range managers, you may be the only wildlife biologist working with animals in a many-square-mile area of millions of acres. Census-taking, another frequent assignment, is often done by airplane, the best way to check changes in the population of ospreys, eagles, and deer. In addition to coordinated efforts with foresters and others, a great deal of the wildlife biologist's work in national forests involves interrelationships with industry, lumbering, and mining in permitted areas, to ensure environmental protection.

The same basic tasks of animal management are performed by wildlife biologists in state forests, national parks, and state parks. In parklands, however, the public is a factor, and the interaction of animals and people—visitors, campers, and hunters—is an important part of maintaining animal well-being through successful management of habitats and control of hunting volume.

Some biologists say half their time is spent in animal observation, banding, and other direct involvement. The other half—and often a higher proportion of time—is taken up with recording, analyzing, and reporting their findings and in related administrative detail.

One biologist whose time was largely taken up with travel was Dr. George Schaller of the New York Zoological Society. Dr. Schaller was a field worker—the ultimate wildlife biologist—and he was also a conservationist and zoologist. He has spent months, even years at a time, in such countries as Brazil, India, and Zaire. His job: researching wild animals and planning wildlife preserves for them.

Much of Dr. Schaller's work was funded by research grants from the National Geographic Society and similar organizations.

A detailed field study—of snow leopards in the Himalayas, for instance—takes two to three years. Although Dr. Schaller worked from a home base as close to the animals as possible and often took his family along to work with him, he spent much time in isolated field work. In Tanzania, his home base was 200 miles from the area he was observing, which meant a lot of tent camping for the biologist.

Dr. Schaller's work was more than pure research into animal habitats and conditions. Part of his goal was to work with local governments to design and establish preserves for protecting the wildlife he studied. He also wrote extensively and worked with wildlife-dedicated assistants in the host countries, teaching them how to conserve their own valuable wildlife.

Some 65 percent of wildlife biologists work for states, 20 percent for the federal government, and the rest for universities, zoos, environmental groups, and foundations. The available jobs usually go to those with advanced degrees. This is true in every area of conservation work, as it is with zoo work. If you want to be competitive, pile on those degrees! Experience helps, too.

Here is a sampling of jobs that may be available in the classifieds section in your newspaper or in a trade magazine:

WETLAND SCIENTIST/BOTANIST. Knowledge of wetland delineation procedures and northwest plant communities. Wetland permitting and delineation experience desirable. Excellent benefits.

WATERFOWL BIOLOGIST M.S. with experience or Ph.D. Good quantitative skills desired. Oversees management and research on waterfowl population and habitat. Supervises biologist and half-time secretary.

WILDLIFE MANAGER I, B.S. in wildlife science; WILDLIFE MANAGER II, B.S. in wildlife science + 2 years professional experience in wildlife management. Biologist/wildlife law enforcement responsible for implementing fish and wildlife population and habitat management.

WILDLIFE SPECIALISTS, B.S. in wildlife science + 2 years experience in wildlife management. Future vacancies anticipated.

DEER PROGRAM LEADER, M.S. in wildlife. Responsible for statewide management and research programs.

SEASONAL RAPTOR SURVEYORS. Two years wildlife experience, preferably with raptors. To survey and monitor goshawks and spotted owls April–August.

BIOLOGICAL TECHNICIANS (4) April 13–September 25. To assist refuge personnel in implementation of biological and management programs including capture and banding of American woodcock using trained bird dogs, modified shorebird traps, mist nets, and nightlighting; waterfowl capture and banding; pellet counts, etc. Housing included.

RANGERS

Rangers are employed by national and state parks. Their duties are similar in both facilities, and there is some overlap with tasks performed by wildlife biologists and wildlife conservation officers.

Park rangers and their supervisors have the most direct control over park lands, the animals who live there, and the visitors who come there. The ranger welcomes visitors, assigns campsites, collects fees, reports on weather conditions, conducts nature walks and campfire lectures, and answers every question from "Will the bears bother me?" to "Where can I get ice?"

The ranger is also a police officer of sorts whose duties include making the public aware of park rules and seeing to it they are obeyed. Where hunting and fishing are permitted, this job is more often done by the wildlife conservation officer.

Another element of ranger life is overseeing the general condition of the park. Are fences mended? Trails neat and well-marked? Parking areas clean? Campsites ready for occupancy? Rangers patrol all areas of the park, noting what work must be done and assigning it to conservation crews, often young seasonal workers or volunteers. Ranger duties may take you far away from the public and may involve long periods out-of-doors, patrolling by 4WD vehicle or on horseback.

Along with the people- and park-care elements of the job, rangers are front-line animal care workers, too. A ranger must have an intimate knowledge of the park's wildlife mixture and the visitors' impact on it, of weather conditions and their potential effects on the animals, and of what steps to take toward successful animal management. Along with the wildlife biologist, the ranger surveys wildlife and reports on its conditions, provides animals with water and food in times of severe weather, rescues animals found in difficulties, and traps animals to move them to distant locations where food supplies are better or where visitors will not go.

The answer to "Will the bears bother me?" might just be "Yes" if conditions are wrong. When bears and other predators cannot find food in the wild, they may raid campsites—not a good state of affairs. By taking positive action in advance, the rangers and their assistants can maintain the proper balance in the park between people and the natural environment.

The forest ranger and range manager are related careers. Forest rangers monitor environmental and man-made conditions in national and state forests. While these duties include a degree of animal care, it is secondary to the overall preservation of forest lands, the control or direction of logging where it is permitted, and the general management of thousands of acres of uninhabited wilderness.

Range managers perform many of the same duties, but in addition they interact with ranchers who may be permitted to use the open rangelands for grazing cattle. The range manager helps determine the amount of grazing that may be done and works with ranchers to maintain the size of the herd and the size and location of available acreage.

Federal government salaries are among the highest for ranger technology. State and local governments pay less. And although local governments offer good fringe benefits such as health insurance, the federal government still offers the best career opportunities overall.

WILDLIFE CONSERVATION OFFICER

Titles such as *wildlife conservation officer, conservation warden* or—most usually in the public mind—*game warden* all describe the same state government position. In federal government work for the U.S. Fish and Wildlife Service the title is *special agent.*

Originally the job was one purely of enforcement of hunting and fishing laws. Today the job still involves the regulation of game animals (mammals, birds, and fishes) including investigation and enforcement, and there is also increasing overlap with the tasks of other conservation workers.

Today, as a wildlife conservation officer, you would check licenses, regulate catches, and enforce applicable laws—but you also may help conduct animal surveys, do rescue work, operate feeding stations, relocate animals, and even be involved in fire detection and monitoring state and private game breeding farms. Like the park ranger, you might speak before civic-minded hunting and fishing groups, providing safety information and emphasizing the need for conservation to their audiences.

Federal special agents are primarily enforcement officers performing a broad range of regulatory duties from granting federal wildlife permits to flying enforcement patrols.

As with growing numbers of conservation workers, education past high school is becoming almost essential as a requirement for the limited number of available jobs. And several states have physical requirements that must be met. Experience in some phases of wildlife management and conservation or law enforcement is decidedly helpful. Federal special agents must have a bachelor's degree in wildlife biology or criminal justice, or at least its equivalent in job-related experience.

SEASONAL WORK, VOLUNTEERING, AND CONSERVATION TEEN CLUBS

You can be a VIP! A "VIP" (volunteer-in-park) is an individual who can offer his or her services in parks across the country. If you are interested in park work, write the National Park Services under the auspices of the U.S. Department of the Interior. Ask them to send you the booklet that represents your geographical region. The regions are: the Alaska Region, the Pacific Northwest Region, the Western Region, the Rocky Mountain Region, the Southwest Region, the Midwest Region, the Southeast Region, the Mid-Atlantic Region, the National Capital Region, and the North Atlantic Region.

In each regional booklet are all the parks, special seashores, monument areas, railroad historical sites, etc., within that geographical area. Under each site are listed the specific things that need to be done. In Maryland, for instance, the Assateague Island National Seashore needs people to work in protection and resource management areas. Other parks have other needs.

How old do you have to be? Well, the good news is that you may help out even if you are under eighteen. Students under eighteen must work at parks in their own communities and have the permission of their parents. If they wish to work elsewhere, they must work *with* their families or with a supervised group.

Other volunteer groups (besides individual teens) are as diverse as park neighbors, college students (who do not have the age limitations just mentioned for high schoolers), farmers, or engineers—almost anyone in any area. The only attributes these groups are required to have are outdoor talent and skills, or, in some cases, simply the desire to learn.

Volunteers work alongside the National Park Service employees. Many of the assignments are not related to animals. But except for city parks or urban historical sites, you will be in woodsy areas where animals and often fish abound. Jobs working closest to animals are: serving as a campground host, maintaining trails, and assisting park managers taking wildlife "head-counts."

If you are truly interested in working in a park, you will fill out a regional application indicating your interests and skills. You may say, for example, that you want to be a veterinarian or a conservationist and that you have taken courses in areas leading to these specializations. In high school, such courses would include biology and the other sciences. The park system will try to match their needs with your interests.

Of course, one of the best reasons for being a VIP is that you will someday be able to list this experience on a job resume in an animal-related field. In the meantime, park volunteering will simply be a wonderful, exciting way to spend your time.

The Humane Society of the United States (HSUS) is an organization you might want to join. As a member, you'll be part of one of the world's largest and most effective organizations fighting to protect animals and the earth. Whether you're concerned about rain forests or pet overpopulation, animal testing or endangered species, the HSUS needs your help.

You can join the organization for $10 per year. For $25 per year, you'll also receive the HSUS's *All Animals,* a quarterly magazine for members. Members can also receive *Humane Activist,* a newsletter about proposed new laws and other actions to help animals and the environment.

For more information about programs for students, write to:

The HSUS Youth Education Division
2100 L Street NW
Washington, DC 20037

Or visit their website at www.hsus.org.

Breed Rescue

One recent HSUS student paper reported on Jeanette Cretara, a biology major at UCLA. In her senior year at high school, Jeanette took on a year-long project to find good, permanent homes for shelter animals. When interviewing some of the prospective owners who responded to her ads in pet supply stores and in newspaper classified ads, she met with disappointment. For example, one potential adopter said all his dogs ran away (they had no I.D. tags). Jeanette's reply was "My foster pets have already been in homes with irresponsible owners. They don't need to be put in those situations again." Here was an animal lover who went beyond the expected to ensure loving care for her pets.

Jeanette Cretara is one of many who work hard in breed rescue. Breed rescue used to be by "word of mouth," but with the Internet, many dogs are saved through a breed rescue chain. One woman, Michele McArdle, has placed more than sixty-five hundred boxers over a period of twenty years. She is on the boxer "grapevine," and it is powerful! The "internetting" is composed of veterinarians, breeders, and happy recipients of boxers. There are expenses, of course, when a member of any breed is placed to cover shots, kenneling, etc.

Another good website is the American Kennel Club. Approximately 134 breeds have rescue service listed on the A.K.C. Their online address is www.akc.org.

Many breeds have their own website. The E-mail of the collie is poignant-irescuecollies@aol.com. The kuvasz is a handsome roly-poly dog and a great guard dog, too. The website for this breed of dog is www.kuvasz.com.

Because of animal lovers like yourself, for many frolicking, happy, and newly placed pups, it doesn't have to be a dog's life!

EARTH AND ANIMAL PROTECTION CLUBS: MAKING A DIFFERENCE*

Not long ago, a group of people dedicated to protecting animals scored a major victory for the endangered African elephant. Their effort began when they learned about the crop destruction caused by elephants that lived near a small village in Kenya. The elephants had been eating almost all the crops grown by the local people. In order to protect their food source, the villagers had no choice but to shoot the huge, hungry animals. Or so it seemed. The animal protection group had a different plan. They knew that if an electric fence was put up to protect the villagers' crops, both the elephants and the crops could be saved.

But there was one problem with the group's scheme: The fence cost $2,000. How could they possibly raise that kind of money in time to save the elephants? Instead of becoming discouraged and giving up, they sprang into action. By designing, silk-screening,

---

*Reprinted with permission from HSUS Student Action Guide.

and selling their own wildlife T-shirts, the group was able to raise enough money to buy the fence. Then, with the help of several people who lived in Kenya, the fence was built and the elephants and the villagers' crops were saved.

Who were the people who did so much in so little time to save the beautiful African elephant? You might think they were members of a big national organization such as The Humane Society of the United States.

But they weren't. They were actually students from Petaluma, California, who had formed their own animal protection group called Friends of Wildlife (FOWL). The kids in FOWL and in many similar groups around the country know that you don't have to be an adult to make a *real* difference in the world. They've learned that with a little heart, hard work, and determination, junior and senior high school students can be a major force in the battle to protect animals and the environment. And that's what this guide is all about. This story shows that you and your classmates can become a force for positive change by forming your own Earth and animal protection club. Whether you want to save the rain forests, protect endangered species, or end the pet overpopulation problem, once you decide to act together, you'll be amazed at how much you can accomplish.

Get the Facts: Information on Controversial Issues Like Trapping

As your club begins planning activities and projects, you may find that it's fairly easy to obtain information about environmental issues from television, books, newspapers, and magazines. But facts about animal protection issues are sometimes more difficult to find. To make your information search a little easier, The HSUS can provide you with fact sheets on the following issues:

puppy mills
dogfighting

horse racing
wild birds
rodeos
horse auctions
donkey basketball
pound seizure
trapping
cockfighting
dog racing
pet overpopulation
the Federal Animal Welfare Act
hunter harassment
factory farming
livestock in stockyards
draize & LD 50 tests (lab animals)

HSUS cites five steps (and their variations) to start a club in your school or neighborhood (i.e., find a knowledgeable school adviser and decide on a specific issue to target) and take action.

Here is an example of an HSUS high school group tackling two of the environmentalists' most sensitive subjects: (1) unusual and unnecessary cruelty to animals, and (2) the fate of the world's dolphins. Five hundred students from Lincoln, Nebraska, were shocked to learn that dolphins died unnecessarily in nets used to catch tuna. The students collected signatures from fellow club members asking that tuna caught in nets also entrapping dolphins not be served for their cafeteria lunches. A prominent tuna company took notice of the signed petition and devised ways to catch tuna without endangering the dolphins.

Have you ever thought that kids can't get anything done? This example and many other HSUS projects prove that kids can make a *great* difference in our environment and in the conservation of our species, endangered or not.

Below are two examples of exciting volunteer jobs. These jobs are generally for adults, but as the second example shows, some of them apply to teens.

VOLUNTEERS. U.S. Fish & Wildlife Service. Early May through August/September. Background in wildlife botany. Prefer field experience. To work in remote area; enthusiasm, teamwork. For diverse field experience in Nevada or Oregon's Great Basin Desert. Riparian bird, waterfowl, bighorn sheep, etc. surveys. Stipend, housing, refuge transportation and equipment provided.

VOLUNTEERS, all ages, abilities to become involved in preservation of Adirondack trail system. Between May and September. Work with native wood, rock, and dirt to maintain and reconstruct badly eroded trail. Full-time seasonal positions also available.

CAREERS IN CONSERVATION

The conservation movement is largely the province of a variety of private foundations and organizations. While some are conservation-minded in a general way, many are single-issue organizations dedicated to preserving such creatures as seals or whales, or to maintaining marshlands or wilderness areas against the onslaught either of commercial animal exploitation or industrial takeover.

Although their financing is a relative drop in the bucket compared to government spending for forests, parks, and wildlife and conservation, the environmental organizations with Washington lobbies wield a surprising amount of influence and throw an increasing number of dollars into the environmental fight.

Not all environmental groups are animal-related; their concerns range from furthering solar energy to fighting corporate pollution.

All of these advocacy groups offer opportunities for caring people, although direct contact with animals is limited at best. (Only super-activist organizations like Greenpeace send people into nature to go literally head-to-head against animal slaughterers.) But they do offer career opportunities for people willing to work for their causes indirectly.

Among these specialists are professional lobbyists whose role is to influence legislators favorably toward their causes, local, regional, and national. Other advocates approach the task through the legal process, studying environmental and animal regulations and working with legislators to create more favorable legislation, to strengthen the laws that exist, and to work against their pro-industry lobbying counterparts.

A major role is fund-raising among individuals and environmentally concerned corporations. People who would ordinarily be involved in the sales and marketing of consumer products and services instead devote their abilities to "selling" the "product" of the environmental group for whom they work, marketing their group's philosophy just as they would any other commodity—with equal skill and dedication.

Within each organization just as in any industrial company are the "troops"—those who create the communications, open the mail, answer the telephones, keep the books, run the computers, and do every other kind of office job—but for a cause they believe to be more important than marketing automobiles or promoting motion pictures.

Not all work, however, is office-based or centered in Washington, DC. The Nature Conservancy (TNC), for instance, although headquartered across the Potomac in Arlington, Virginia, is a vast organization that now owns many nature preserves nationwide. But land ownership and management is not its primary goal. TNC has been extremely successful in buying open land and reselling it to dedicated corporations that are as intent on its preservation as the conservancy. TNC also markets land to local environmental groups, which repay its cost through private fund-raising. It has acquired land that it has turned over to many states under similar preservation arrangements. So far, the influential organization has saved several million acres.

TNC deeply feels its responsibilities in managing the land it owns. It employs a corps of environmental and wildlife biologists, range and land managers, and enforcement people. Their training and work are very similar to the jobs performed in state and national preserves: maintaining the balance of nature; preserving endangered species; and controlling hunting, fishing, and camping in lands where these activities are permitted. TNC employs corporate and individual fund-raisers, land acquisition specialists, and others whose business is preserving the past to protect the future.

TNC also welcomes volunteers, as does any nonprofit corporation or environmental group. Volunteering your time and talent may well be a way to acquire experience that will eventually pay off in preservation- or animal-related employment.

Volunteering can be equally rewarding for the professional who can give of time and ability. The late Marlin Perkins was one such passionate animal protectionist. The Director Emeritus of the St. Louis Zoo and co-producer of the acclaimed TV series, *Wild Kingdom,* Perkins was a highly vocal and effective advocate of animal protection. He defended the modern zoo, citing numerous examples of the zoo's role in preventing the extinction of many species, and criticized shortsighted policies such as the wholesale slaughter of wolves. With the wolves largely gone, problems such as overabundance of elk in places like Yellowstone National Park have been the result. So strongly did Marlin Perkins feel on this subject that he and his wife, Carol, worked to create a natural sanctuary for wolves just a few miles from their St. Louis home.

Dr. Harold Albers, a Florida veterinarian and past president of the Pinellas County Veterinary Medical Association, has become an expert on the treatment of oil-damaged waterfowl, and contributes his time and knowledge at many conferences on this and other aspects of animal management. He has involved oil companies in the problem with excellent results, and he has developed a bird re-habilitation manual now widely used by groups such as Florida's Associated Marine Institutes and International Bird Rescue. With nine thousand miles of coastland requiring preservation and protection with limited funds, the state of Florida needs the help of dedicated people like Dr. Albers.

COMMUNICATIONS

There are varied opportunities in communications for the animal care worker, although these are often combined with other duties.

In both national and state parks, the park rangers develop and conduct tours, lectures, and nature walks that usually emphasize wildlife and conservation. They may also create and produce park information leaflets, brochures, and tourist information to distribute to park visitors.

In zoos and safari parks, especially those catering to children, assistant curators or skilled animal keepers may prepare live animal exhibits and also run a children's zoo. Nearly every zoo also has a public relations person who writes brochures and prepares talks on the animals. These same people, or other staffers, may be animal photographers who prepare the pictures for slide shows, publicity releases, and brochures.

Conservation organizations also use the services of skilled communications people who prepare fund-raising and consciousness-raising materials for direct mail solicitation and awareness programs. Some organizations have staff people to prepare communications while others either share this responsibility with outside advertising and public relations firms, or turn all such work over to them.

Although they are relatively rare, there are full-time journalists and photographers whose careers are largely or entirely concerned with animals.

Competition is keen for just about all communications assignments. Since the communications person may have to wear other organizational hats as well, your possibilities of working in animal communications are improved if you have excellent writing and verbal skills. It also helps to have a thorough art knowledge (layout and design and/or desktop publishing), plus photographic or illustrative capabilities. Finally, it is important to know the animals you'll work with and make a good impression on the public with a well-developed ability to talk on your feet.

World Society for the Protection of Animals

John C. Walsh is a man with a mission. As the international projects director of the London-based World Society for the Protection of Animals (WSPA), Walsh travels the world to save animals at risk.

Animals suffering from the aftereffects of volcanos, floods, and wars around the world are the recipients of WSPA's skillful care, as are those in need of help closer to home.

Take tigers, for instance. Tigers in New Jersey! A woman keeping seven tigers was unaware that one of her large, fang-toothed creatures had gotten loose. Although the tiger ultimately was shot, the lady was judged to be handling her "pets" in a humane way. Just as well. "It's not easy to find a truck that will haul tigers," Walsh commented dryly.

Walsh and his staff are at almost every natural disaster—and unnatural ones, too.

In the aftermath of the Persian Gulf War, Walsh was asked by the Saudi Arabian government to lead a team of scientists and volunteers on an animal rescue mission. In this case, a massive oil spill begun by Iraqi soldiers was a man-made disaster. Walsh and his team were able to capture and clean many types of wildlife that otherwise would have perished, later releasing them into safer habitats.

Once the city of Kuwait was secured by U.S. troops, Walsh made a trip to the National Zoo there, only to be confronted with a dismal situation. Iraqi soldiers had not only neglected the animals by neither feeding nor cleaning them, in several cases animals had actually been tortured. An elephant had been shot in the shoulder, the bullet left in the festering wound. A bear had been beaten with pipes. Two hippos, having been left for months in a habitat never cleaned of its increasing layer of filth, suffered significant skin damage. Many animals had not survived.

Walsh recruited American soldiers as volunteers and set about healing the remaining animals. They fed the animals fresh water, scrambled eggs, and just as important, caring companionship, a healing gift for both animals and humans in such painful circumstances.

When Hurricane Mitch whipped through the Honduras in 1998, Walsh sent huge amounts of supplies to help the animals, including seventeen tons of horse and cattle food and wagon loads of nourishing meals for pigs and dogs.

Medical supplies were also in great demand. Polluted water caused respiratory problems and foot rot. Because of this, veterinary surgeons from the Angell Memorial Hospital in Boston flew to Honduras to make some inroads into the animal crisis by providing vital antibiotics and care.

Are there paying jobs in assisting Mr. Walsh and others in their humane efforts? Indeed there are. But those seeking this exciting work need to have some hands-on experience. Veterinarians, veterinary technicians, and "wrangler"-types for rounding up runaway livestock are what Mr. Walsh and his team have in mind.

The website for the World Society for the Protection of Animals is www.wspa.org.uk. or call 1-800-883-WSPA.

JOB OUTLOOK

Career opportunities for rangers, conservation scientists, and others in the wildlife fields are strong. This is partly due to a wave of retirements in the field and a decline in the number of people going into the wildlife area.

Jobs are still not keeping pace with some other animal areas due to limited government budgets; however, open or public rangeland still needs to be protected. And private industry has shown far greater interest in employing conservationists. Also, owners of range and grazing land need conservation scientists to advise them. Landowners are looking for ways to improve their land for the encouragement of wildlife procreation as well as animal herd health.

CHAPTER 13

CAREERS WITH DOGS: FROM PAMPERED PET TO GUARD DOG

Man's best friend offers many opportunities for young people to carve interesting careers. Dogs now enjoy "dog hotels," day care centers, gourmet bakeries, and customized dog walking. Almost everyone starting in the field works for someone else, but experience, initiative, a developing business sense, and an ability to get along well with people can result in a successful career working for yourself. Many are the dog groomers, kennel assistants, or veterinary hospital aides who have gone on to establish their own boarding kennels, obedience schools, or professional handling clientele.

COMBINATION CAREERS

The primary dog-related careers are kennel owner, breeder, groomer, trainer, and handler. Many people combine two or more areas of expertise in a single career. A kennel owner may board and groom dogs for customers and may also breed dogs for sale or conduct obedience classes for dogs and their owners.

As we discuss the careers individually, keep in mind the possibilities of combining one or more—one career alone may not provide enough income.

Remember, too, that all dog-related careers call for a high degree of "that special something" we've mentioned earlier: the innate, almost instinctive ability to relate strongly to animals, to understand them and in turn to be understood (and not be fooled!) by them. Dogs, like other creatures, know almost instantly, as little children do, who is on their wavelength and who is not. Professional "dog people" are almost universal in their belief that this trait is a gift rather than something that can be learned; either you have it or you don't. Even limited experience with dogs will point the way for you in this respect.

EDUCATIONAL AND PHYSICAL REQUIREMENTS

Much dog-related activity is learned by doing, although there are a few schools that offer training in such areas as dog grooming and kennel management. The best way to learn is to start as an apprentice or helper to someone in one of the career areas. High school courses in biology and the natural sciences are a help, as is a basic understanding of animal health. Happy experience with your own dog is a good beginning, too.

There are some physical demands. Lots of work is involved. Large dogs can be hefty and cumbersome—and they won't climb onto their own three-foot-high grooming tables!

KENNEL WORK—THE ENTRÉE

Working in a breeding or boarding kennel is probably the best entrée to any career with dogs. As a kennel worker, you may be short on money, but you can expect to be long on experience—kennel work is the closest thing to total canine immersion.

The things you do will be varied. You may be called upon to prepare dry dog food or cut up meat for meals; keep cages and runs clean and fresh; fill water bowls, exercise the dogs, help with nail-clipping, brushing, and washing and grooming chores; and answer the telephone. If yours is a boarding kennel, you may also sign in visiting pets, record and collect their boarding fees, note their food preferences, write down where their owners can be reached in case of emergency, and check the pets out when they are departing.

If you work for a breeding kennel you can expect, in addition to all the customary kennel chores, to assist with breeding and birthing, and perhaps to show puppies to prospective buyers. If yours is a kennel that teaches obedience courses or is involved in the dog show circuit, you may help with the training classes or go along on the busy weekend show tours. This job means hours of driving or flying, taking care of the pets en route, helping with their grooming on arrival at the show, and packing everything up again for the trip home, or to the next show—some exhibitors attend two shows in one weekend.

You could be doing all of the above—indeed, total immersion!

In the process, there's a lot to know, and you would be learning it the best possible way: under the watchful eyes of those who know the subject intimately and who would have something new to teach you almost every hour of the day. You would learn the finer points of removing burrs from a dog's shaggy coat and perhaps the ins-and-outs of dog obedience training. You may learn what the proper conformation (physical characteristics and appearance) should be for one or more breeds, and what show judges look for, in ring judging and obedience trials, from the dog and its handler. You'd learn the basics of dog feeding and care, and at least some of the rudiments of veterinary medicine and the recognition of dog health problems. You would soon catch on to what kennel temperatures are right for different breeds—room temperature for most small dogs, lower for outdoor breeds—and the right way to get a dog to swallow a pill.

Most important, you would learn whether operating a kennel is your idea of a lifetime career, or if more specialized work with dogs is best for you.

Harris Dunlap's Zero Kennels

Harris Dunlap of Bakers Mills, New York, is a kennel operator whose hobby—racing sled dogs—became the basis for his career. His Zero Kennels, which he operates as a family business, is the largest associated with this unique sport.

Dunlap's interest began shortly after he finished his college training as an artist. He bought a Siberian husky as a pet and added a war surplus dogsled. His activity has grown with the sport, which has boomed in the last twenty-five years. Now, Harris Dunlap wins prize money in dogsled races and earns considerably more by breeding, training, and selling his own breed of sled dogs.

Racing sled dogs is a rugged life, especially in the one hundred-day racing season that starts every New Year's Day. Dunlap and his teams may travel 20,000 miles in this time to compete in races as long as 1,171 miles that are held in winter settings as far away as Alaska. His usual entourage is thirty-six racing dogs plus sleds, equipment, and crew. Each dog is well fed and well rested between races.

Dunlap's own dogs, which he spends the rest of the year breeding and training, are specially bred by him for racing. The breed is based on the Siberian husky, but other traits have been bred in, vascular strength and stamina, for instance. Stamina is the essential element of the sled dog: Each dog runs about one thousand five hundred miles in training and competition during the racing season. Of his thirty-six racing dogs, twenty are lead dogs, extra-intelligent animals capable of interpreting the driver's wishes to the team dogs by a combination of instinct and example. Because the mental and physical pressures are considerable, the lead dogs are rotated frequently, but never during a race. Race rules have it that dogs may be removed from a team but new ones cannot be substituted.

The Kennel Business

As a beginning kennel worker, you would need no financial investment for a salaried job. As you gain experience, a bit of paid time off, occasional bonuses for extra hours worked, and even a profit-sharing arrangement may come your way.

A salaried, experienced kennel worker employed full-time and with living accommodations provided may earn a comfortable living.

If you decide to operate your own kennel, you will have to scout for a suitable location to buy or rent in an area where kennels are acceptable and decide which canine services you should offer. What you earn will be governed by your overhead versus your charges for the services you give and the volume your kennel attracts. A good business sense and an outgoing personality, important to the kennel worker, are essential ingredients for success in your own kennel business.

DOG GROOMER

Debbie Weiss, owner and sole operator of Debbie's Dog Grooming Salon in Elkins Park, Pennsylvania, finds her work very creative. "A dog may come here in a total mess," she says. "I groom him and make him feel better." This is her motivation—her work makes *her* feel good, too.

Creating what she calls "creature comfort" is not easy. A total grooming involves careful combing-out of the coat—often with considerable thinning and clipping—as the first step. Nails may be clipped, too, something many dogs fail to appreciate while it's going on. Nor do they relish ear-cleaning. Then it's into the bath, and the reaction to this depends on the dog. Some love it, others express different opinions! After a thorough, careful drying—often done with drying equipment that dries the fur but does not dry out the skin or allow the dog to become chilled—comes further brushing, thinning, clipping, and styling. The final touch may be a bit of scent, and the job is done.

A dog groomer may operate an independent business as Debbie does, or work for a kennel owner or in a grooming salon. Since it's strictly "piece work," volume is the key to making it work financially. Since overhead—rent, heat, light, and advertising—are fixed expenses, the grooming operation not associated with a kennel has to be brisk to be successful. A groomer who works for a kennel may be in a fairly good position since there are always other things to do if the grooming part of the business is slow.

The groomer who works for an established shop usually does so on commission, much as a hairstylist does. This is normally 50 percent of what the shop charges the customer; thus, earnings will vary with the shop's volume.

Opening a grooming shop means that you as owner can earn more than you could as an employee. But doing so also means making an investment for signs, reception area, grooming tables and tools, cages, driers, rent deposit, and utility connection charges—plus, of course, the continuing overhead expenses. Shop owners say that among the elements needed for success are an accessible location in a busy neighborhood with easy parking and a consistent advertising program. A good listing in the Yellow Pages is mentioned by many. If you have established a good reputation as a groomer with another nearby kennel or salon, you may have some built-in following when you open your doors. Your chances would be even better if you were lucky enough to be able to buy out or buy into a going shop, perhaps the one for which you work.

One of the few schools for dog grooming in the country is in Philadelphia. The Pennsylvania School of Dog Grooming is licensed by the state and offers basic, advanced, and professional courses for "...that special someone with a lot of patience and a great love and compassion for animals." Another school, this one in California, offers a fifteen-week course with a total of six hundred classroom hours. Live—often lively—subjects, including an occasional cat, are used to teach every element of the craft.

TRAINING CAREERS

In addition to their value as pets, many dogs are bred and trained for work. Others are trained just to be nicer to have around—no unscheduled barking, jumping into laps, or bedroom-slipper breakfasts. And many dogs are carefully trained for performance in the show ring and the obedience trial field. While some canine skills are instinctive—sheepdogs, for instance, seem to be born knowing what to do with sheep—most must be taught by people.

Different training goals call for specific knowledge, but all dog trainers have many traits in common. Their patience, for one thing, must be almost infinite. Dogs are highly intelligent and retain knowledge well once it is given to them, but the giving calls for extreme patience plus consistency and kindness. Firmness, too, is part of the trainer's makeup, but firmness always applied in a gentle and consistent way. Dogs thrive on appreciation; even when a dog does something wrong and is made to understand this, the impression from the trainer must be a kindly one. Experienced dog trainers can earn $25 to $125 an hour, depending upon how many dogs are "clients" at a given time.

The Leader Dog Trainers

Almost all trainers, whether schooling dogs in obedience, training them to lead the blind, or to be part of a law enforcement team, must be people-oriented as well as animal-oriented. This is certainly true of the twenty full-time trainers (among a staff of fifty-six) who work at the headquarters of Leader Dogs for the Blind® of Rochester, Michigan.

Leader Dogs for the Blind is funded primarily by the Lions International, a service organization dedicated to aiding the blind. Even the dogs are contributed. They are usually German shepherds and labrador and golden retrievers, and are always female, because they have proved to be more temperamentally suited to the work than males.

When the dogs arrive at Rochester, they are trained for five months by the trainers. As part of their own training, the trainers are often blindfolded, to appreciate firsthand what it is like to be dependent on a dog for guidance.

A dog to be trained as a Leader Dog will first learn to wear the shoulder harness that is its contact with the blind person. The dog must learn that she's "on duty" whenever this harness is in place. One by one, with constant repetition, the instructor repeats the commands that the blind person will use and teaches the dog the correct response to each one. The dog is taught to stop, to go forward, and to go right or left on command. Most important, it is taught to stop at every curb, even the wheelchair curbs that are flush with the street. In time, the dogs learn not to go forward into traffic—but the blind owner must take the responsibility for the dog's reactions to commands; that is, the owner must listen for vehicles and learn to sense the flow of people around her or him in city traffic and thus know when streets can be crossed. This work takes time and infinite patience—small wonder that training the guide dog takes several months before it it is ready to meet its new owner.

Thirty-two human candidates at a time live at the Leader Dog facility and work closely and harmoniously with their dogs and trainers. After a get-acquainted period, the match of dog and candidate is evaluated by the trainer.

The "schooling" of the new owner takes four weeks. First, the dog learns that total allegiance goes not to the trainer whom she knows but to the new master whom she does not. The dog learns, too, that she can relax and simply be a pet and companion when the shoulder harness is replaced with a leash. Work time is over, and the command words for duty are never used when the dog is out of harness. Dog and master live as one during the training.

Every day, in good weather and bad—Leader Dog applicants are forewarned about winter Michigan weather!—dog, master, and trainer practice the commands and movements over and over. A major lesson is learning to respond to the master's commands. As confidence grows, candidates, trailed discreetly by the trainers, move from the grounds of the Leader Dog facility into the small-town traffic of Rochester. Traffic situations are slowly added as familiarity and confidence are established, and before "graduation," the rush of nearby Detroit traffic is taken in stride. The trainers teach city-bound dogs and owners to cope with such special conditions as elevators, revolving doors, train and bus steps, and subway stations.

Dogs are taught never to cross streets diagonally but only from one curb to the opposing one—a degree of consistency that is essential to the blind person's confidence in maintaining proper orientation in city traffic.

In an article, "Free to Travel," Leader Dog training is explained this way: "The orientation and mobility program...deals with the areas of body image, gait, coordination, position and awareness of location. The...program attempts to look at each person as an individual, assess the handicap, and plan a program to insure effective and efficient travel."

It is the trainer's responsibility to train the candidate just as completely as he or she trains the dog so the two become a team. More than three hundred teams are trained each year; more than sixty-four hundred have graduated since the school's founding in 1939.

Once on their own, the dog is "guided" by the blind person to the extent that he or she knows how many streets to cross, and in which direction, to get from point A to point B, and to return. In time and with practice, dog and owner can follow the same course to and from work or from home to the neighborhood store, with a pleasantly relaxed interdependence. In one sense, the training never ends.

Another never-ending consideration is the relationship of dog and master. Leader Dogs for the Blind and similar organizations teach the new masters the same degree of kindness and consistency to which the dogs respond during training—and they usually follow-up afterward to see how the relationship is progressing. Most of the dog and master teams adjust well—a tribute to the quality of the trainers' work and the dedication of all concerned.

Any blind person over age sixteen with the ability and temperament to care for a dog is eligible for a Leader Dog. There is no charge; the cost for each dog and its training is paid for by donations, primarily from Lions Club chapters.

Although it is the largest organization of its kind, Leader Dogs for the Blind is one of several devoted to training dogs for blind people. The Seeing Eye and International Guiding Eyes are two others.

Jobs as trainers of dogs for the blind are neither plentiful nor well-paying. Apprenticeship to a recognized organization is the usual method of entering this specialized training field. Most apprentices should have had at least a year of previous work experience in another area of dog management, as a veterinary assistant, kennel worker, or obedience trainer. Since the job calls for instilling confidence in the dogs and their masters, you as a trainer must have confidence in yourself and be as dedicated to people as you are to animals. Apprenticeships may last as long as three years.

One way in which you could contribute to this cause is to raise a donor pup through the 4-H Club program (see Chapter 4). After a year or more of home life, the 4-H dogs are given to The Seeing Eye in Morristown, NJ.

The K-9 Dog Trainer

The relatively new Canine Companions for Independence, in Bucks County, Pennsylvania, has slightly different goals for its young trainers. The dogs are raised as service dogs aiding the wheelchair bound or others with physical disabilities. A "facility dog" can also go into a day care center or nursing home to cheer the patients. And to serve the handicapped who choose to remain at home, these four-footed helpers can remove laundry from a washer and place it in the dryer! The national website for this organization is www.caninecompanions.org.

Rarer than lead dogs are rescue dogs—dogs that traverse the world in search of disaster victims.

Caroline Hebard of Bernardsville, New Jersey, was the cofounder and leader of the U.S. Disaster and Response Team. She carries a beeper and a duffel bag, ready to go anywhere in the world at a moment's notice. Her rescue dogs are trained from the time they are puppies to perform search and rescue. They learn the signals of victim alarm—wagging their tails if the victim is alive, moving the tail slowly if the person is dying, letting it droop if the victim is dead. The dogs wear orange vests emblazoned with a rescue white cross.

Caroline Hebard and her rescue dogs have assisted at earthquakes, hurricanes, and other natural disasters. Caroline herself risks death as she challenges mud slides, killer bees, and looters with guns. Her life is definitely not a boring one!

German shepherds, diligent, responsive, and intelligent in their work with the blind, exhibit these tendencies—plus a few others—in police work. The K-9 trainer, like the guide dog trainer, works with young, grown dogs, teaching them to wade head-first into trouble—but only on command! The police dog trainer works at the same time to train the police officer who will be the dog's teammate throughout its law enforcement career. This takes place only after the dog has been thoroughly screened to make sure it is not gun-shy—or worse—crowd-shy.

It took fourteen weeks of training before Abington Township (Pennsylvania) police officers Douglas Mealo and Robert Mann and their dogs, Zak and Duke, graduated from the nearby Philadelphia Police Academy with K-9 credentials. Both officers quickly proved the value of their dogs. Officer Mealo and Zak headed off what their commanding officer characterized as "a potential riot" just by appearing before an unruly mob. Officer Mann did even better on a similar occasion: The sound of Duke's barking and the sight of the police van rocking were enough to convince a crowd that it suddenly had better places to be. In investigating a reported home robbery, Zak found—and held—two suspects under a bed until Officer Mealo could arrest them.

As is the custom with K-9 dogs, Zak and Duke live with their officers. The two suburban Philadelphia policemen agree with other K-9 officers that their love of animals was the reason they volunteered for K-9 duty.

The fourteen-week K-9 course given by the Philadelphia Police Academy for its own officers and those of nearby towns is typical. Officer and dog learn together. A command such as "Watch 'em" or "Bark" is the dog's cue to act aggressively—to snarl, bark, bare its teeth, and strain at its leash. Unless commanded to be aggressive, K-9 dogs are alert but quiet and well-mannered. By contrast, they will actually attack when commanded to do so if the officer thinks the situation calls for it.

As with dogs for the blind, the early part of the training is taken up with building mutual confidence between officer and dog—and making sure before the training gets too far that the chemistry is right between them—a job that calls for acute observation and experience on the trainer's part. Then, as with the blind, command and response are replayed until commands are obeyed instantly, consistently, and dependably.

After the teams start police duty, the dogs are kept sharp by continued training in procedures taught by the academy trainers. There may be a period each day or two when officers and their dogs practice attack procedures, with other officers playing the parts of criminal suspects. Since the dogs are taught never to attack someone in uniform, padded jackets are the "uniforms" worn by the "criminals" during these exercises.

Bubba is a friendly Labrador retriever. He is also one of seven dogs trained by the Pennsylvania State Police (the division of the Bureau of Emergency and Special Operations) to sniff out drugs.

When on duty, Bubba wears a handsome state trooper patch. (Bubba, and others like him, are now wearing body armor to prevent injuries on duty.) He and his trainer, state police corporal Karl Grill, have searched airports, ships, and suspicious cars. With their trainers, Bubba and other state police dogs have led to drug seizures of well over fifty million dollars in Pennsylvania.

The training for dogs like Bubba starts with retrieving towels scented with marijuana. Pseudococaine also perfumes towels that are thrown into high grass and other difficult places to retrieve. Soon Bubba and his compatriots are ready for the real thing, and their incredible success in sniffing out drugs or suspects is proof of their effectiveness.

Despite the cost of the dogs and their training and the time away from active duty needed to train a K-9 team, more police departments are realizing the benefits of K-9 patrols. A K-9 team can control even a large crowd far more effectively than several officers—and with far less chance of trouble.

K-9 dog trainers are schooled in basic obedience training, plus the specifics of their police role. Some K-9 dogs are trained on contract by people who raise and train security dogs. And the opportunity to become a K-9 police officer is another potential career with dogs.

Security Dog Trainers

Security dogs are a related specialty, but their training is not as comprehensive as K-9 training. These, too, are usually the breeds that most people are a bit wary of encountering: German shepherds and Dobermans. They are generally not trained to attack, but are schooled to bark and snarl ferociously when approached by someone other than their owner on the property they are guarding. Some, however, are trained to attack.

Security dogs are sometimes rented by the companies that use them. The kennel owner-trainer who specializes in security dogs has a long day. It starts with picking up the dogs in the morning when the factories, lumberyards, or stores where the dogs patrol are about to open, returning them to their kennels, and feeding and caring for them. Through the day when the security dogs sleep, the trainer may work with new dogs or teach obedience classes. As evening approaches, the guard dogs go back to their respective locations for another night of duty.

Although the dogs don't patrol, they don't snooze on the job, either. Their hearing is so acute that they can swiftly and noisily respond to any sound.

The kennel operator who gives rented security dogs their basic training may also be a supplier of trainable or partially trained dogs to police departments. This businessperson may also sell security dogs—again, usually the breeds that people tend to distrust—to people who believe they need the protection of such dogs at home or on a lonely city job. Or such a person can train clients' dogs in security techniques or general obedience.

A dog obedience trainer may also hold classes for dogs and their owners without involving themselves in the overhead and responsibilities of kennel operation. Some trainers are able to operate with little business overhead beyond advertising expense and the cost of renting a hall or gym, or an open field. Others operate kennels or work for kennel owners.

DOG BREEDER

The American Kennel Club (AKC) recognizes 128 distinct dog breeds. Not everyone who buys a purebred dog is interested in showing it—the vast majority just want a good pet with certain characteristics—but the whole dog show scene is big business. From the prestigious Westminster, which could be called the Show of Shows, on down to local events, AKC-sanctioned dog shows attract thousands of exhibitors and their would-be champion dogs. The action is nonstop; a breeder could attend one or two shows every weekend of the year.

The dog breeder whose stock earns the blue ribbons and silver trophies naturally commands far more money for puppies than the one who does not win in competition or who chooses not to compete at all.

The keys to breeding success are a knowledge of breed bloodlines and conformation and the ability to produce puppies in a healthy environment. Acquiring breeding knowledge takes time and experience, usually with one breed, sometimes with two or more. For each mating, the bloodlines and ancestry of past generations on both sides must be studied with care. All past champions are considered in light of the laws of heredity. Since these laws are not absolute, judgment enters the picture: "How good a litter would we get if we bred Champion Lilli von Austerlitz of Grandview with our Champion Ludwig von Wienerschnitzel?" The hope, of course, would be a litter of pups at least some of which would exhibit the finest characteristics of both parents, and all of which would be eminently marketable to dachshund fanciers.

As a dog breeder who tackles the show circuit, you must be prepared to spend a considerable amount of time and money to compete. The show drill involves infinitely careful feeding and grooming of the dogs to be shown—grooming that begins well before the exhibition and continues up to the second before the handler (who may or may not be the breeder-owner) parades the dog for its magic moment before the judges. The dogs must be carefully caged for transport, fed, tended, and kept at their peak en route. And detailed training in show etiquette must take place before a dog is exhibited for the first time.

There's an interesting analogy between dog shows and vintage automobile exhibitions, a subject the authors know firsthand. Just as a classic car must be shown in as close to its original, as-new condition as possible with points deducted from a theoretical one hundred score for flaws spotted by the judges, a show dog must appear to be as close to the ideal example of its breed as possible. And, just as a car owner-exhibitor may feel a certain judge doesn't know Auburn 851 upholstery pleats as well as he or she should, dog exhibitors, too, may complain about judging results. The AKC is working to establish written qualification tests for judges; these have not existed until now. To make the analogy complete, there are no written tests for vintage car judges, either.

But, complaints aside, judges are licensed by AKC and they know the breeds they are asked to judge. Although some may have quirks of subjective judgment that add a factor of luck to judging, the vast majority are qualified and fair.

Even though a dog breeder may choose not to show, a professional works to maintain quality through careful selection—always with AKC-registered stock—to ensure continuity of the breed and satisfaction for buyers.

Dog breeding can be a home industry for the family that mates its AKC-registered female with a similarly registered male and then sells its purebred puppies. These pups come from home or top-rated kennels. But home- or kennel-based breeders all customarily provide the AKC registration for their puppies and raise them in healthy surroundings. Puppies should be kept until well past weaning time and should be wormed, inoculated, and declared healthy by a veterinarian before being offered for sale.

A dog breeder who operates a kennel, or a kennel operator of any kind, must comply with local zoning. Dogs may have to be kept indoors after certain hours, and noise may have to be controlled. For this reason, many kennel owners are in the country or suburbs, and those that primarily sell puppies find this is not a deterrent to business. Nearness to a community is, however, a prerequisite for a kennel that is run primarily for boarding and grooming.

SHOW DOG HANDLER

This is a glamor career with dogs—but behind the glitter lies the grit: long hours, much travel, lengthy apprenticeship, and detailed knowledge.

Any AKC member in good standing can, of course, show his or her own dog in the ring or in obedience trials. But just as the owners of a racehorse hire a jockey to ride for the winner's circle because he's the best, so owners of championship dogs turn over their leashes to professional handlers who often have what it takes to bring out the best there is in a dog.

The leading three hundred or so handlers are members of the Professional Handler's Association, a select organization with its own standards of ethics and performance. Members must have had at least five years' professional handling experience, must publish handling fees for their clients, and must have high personal and financial standing.

A skilled handler can experience great financial rewards, but he or she works hard for it. A handler can travel to one hundred or more shows a year, ranging from Canada to South America and anywhere in the United States.

The handler who takes clients' dogs on each trip is entirely responsible for their care and grooming beforehand, en route, during the show, and on the return.

In addition to having the "certain something" that commands both love and respect from dogs, you as a handler must have "done time"—years of it—in dog obedience, grooming, nutrition, and health care. Many handlers also operate kennels, often with obedience schools as part of the operation.

A few handlers are obedience specialists, working with dogs that may not have the conformation to do well in the show ring, but animals that have the "heart" and intelligence to score high in obedience trials. Most handlers specialize in show judging, working skillfully and smoothly in the ring to give the judges the most advantageous view of the client's dog as possible. A skilled handler makes a dog come across as the best among equals. Many a dog owes the letters "Ch." (Champion) before its name to the person on the business end of the leash.

Handling is a learn-by-doing job, almost invariably an out-growth of earlier skills in obedience training and grooming. Professional handlers view themselves as creative people, able to transform, even inspire, an ungainly animal to become an almost charismatic work of art by the steps they take before the show and the moves they make in the ring. They pride themselves on the payoff that comes from infinite attention to detail.

CHAPTER 14

HORSE FEVER: CAREERS WORKING WITH HORSES

A pronounced affliction strikes many young people from eight to twelve and often lasts to the late teen years, or for life. Its name: "horse fever." If you have it, you know all the symptoms—and you probably enjoy every one!

Whether the ailment can, or should, form the basis of a career with horses is another matter, one that particularly has to do with money. Unless you have a good bit of it, or are willing to work long and hard for very little of it, you may be better off riding horses than raising them or otherwise involving yourself with them financially.

Yet for the apt and dedicated victim of horse fever, there are many career opportunities. Keep in mind (as we mentioned with dog careers) that success may well depend on having a variety of talents. Your chances for eventual financial success are better if you generalize rather than specialize. This rule can, of course, be broken by the truly skilled specialist. But please keep the concept of combining your talents in mind as you read about these separate horse careers.

HORSE BREEDER

It is appropriate to begin equine careers with the one specialty that makes all the others possible. Although fossils from millions of years ago show that America once had horses, there were none when Columbus arrived. The Spanish explorers DeSoto and Coronado brought the first horses to this country. The wild horses of the American West are believed to have descended from them or from those brought to our shores by seventeenth century Spanish missionaries. The colonists brought horses, too, and it was then that breeding became a career. Today's horse breeder is a "descendant" of sorts from—among other famous Americans—George Washington.

Horse breeding generally calls for more formal education and money than most other equine careers. The breeder needs to know the nature and characteristics of the horses being bred—and there are many distinct breeds within the classifications of pony, light horse, and draft horse. The breeder must have a working knowledge of: nutritious feeding practices; selection of stallions and mares for breeding (genetics); safe foaling (birthing); healthy stabling conditions; horse exercise needs; equine diseases and first aid; safe horse transportation; good record-keeping and sound business practices; and marketing knowledge—where and how to advertise, proper pricing, good salesmanship.

These are the things that protect the breeder's profit. Considering the hefty investment needed in horses, pastureland, buildings, feeds, employees, vans, and veterinary fees, making a profit calls for careful attention to every detail.

For every famous racing stable with its outstanding winners, there are scores of others that do not make a profit, so chancy is thoroughbred racing. Many successful horse breeders prefer to pass up the high-rolling in favor of breeding sound, saleable ponies and light (pleasure) horses that are honestly represented and sold at fair prices. Understandably, many horse breeders not only breed and raise horses for sale, but offer the other services such as boarding and riding instruction covered in this chapter, to make their considerable investment pay on a daily basis.

How does the horse breeder learn to evaluate mares and stallions as producers of quality foals? Experience as a horse farm employee is the best way for you to start, but formal education in high school and beyond, at a land grant or agricultural college, is recommended. Many multicurriculum colleges also offer the courses you will need. High school and college courses should include animal husbandry, animal science, biology, business management, economics, farm management, genetics, and the basics of animal health and veterinary medicine.

From a start in agricultural or vo-tech high school and membership in a 4-H Club or Future Farmers of America chapter, you could work on a horse farm during summers and between semesters at college. Considering the relatively low pay, it may take time to save enough to buy your first mare to breed or stallion to place at stud, but that should be your goal.

With all the variables of expense versus income, it is hard to say what a horse breeder can earn from her or his entrepreneurial business...but the better the breeding involved, the higher the price of the product. The hours of outdoor work are long, and the challenges are considerable. They are offset by having the breeding farm as your country home and by the daily joy of living, working with, and developing your own horses.

STABLE OWNER AND RIDING INSTRUCTOR

Kate Goldenberg, a Bedminster, Pennsylvania, riding instructor and stable owner, believes that most self-owned animal businesses are expensive propositions. "In my work, fencing, grain, safety features on stalls—all these cost money. And if you don't have quality, people won't board with you. They have to trust you to care for their animals."

As riding instructor, trainer, breeder, and horse farm manager, Kate is aware of this faith placed in her. For her, animal care is a full-time job that cuts no corners. Make that a twenty-four-hour job—mares have a tendency to foal at night!

Kate also sees her field in terms of intrinsic rewards. "There may be a satisfaction in getting rich," she says, "but if you look out over your beautiful farm and animals and don't have a penny in your pocket, you are rich." Like many professionals, Kate cautions: "Don't confuse an affection for horses with an aptitude for working with them. Do stable work, either as a volunteer or for a little pay, to make sure you're up to the demands that animals make—they can be confining."

Like most people who operate riding facilities for profit, Kate Goldenberg offers a variety of services, from boarding others' horses to giving lessons and leading trail rides with her own animals—even staging horse shows on her farm. Kate is of the school that teaches do it right, or not at all. A damp, drafty stable, an over-age horse van, and inadequate cleaning, feeding, exercise, and grooming will cost more in equine ill-health and other problems than such short-cutting will save.

Volunteering is the best way to get your feet muddy (if not wet) in the horse world. Working with an experienced stable operator, you'll learn how to ride for pleasure and for show; how to groom, saddle, and feed horses; how to treat simple ailments that do not need a veterinarian's attention—and how to recognize troubles that do. As a start, you may muck out the horses' stalls, that never-ending job that gave Hercules fits at the Augean stables! But mucking, like every other chore, goes with the territory.

One very worthwhile task for the volunteer and the dedicated stable owner is giving riding lessons to the handicapped, also called therapeutic riding. Although the idea is relatively new, it is growing in popularity. Most participating organizations are members of NARHA, the North American Riding for the Handicapped Association. NARHA supervises therapeutic riding programs to see that their safety standards and teaching methods are followed.

Only gentle, specially schooled horses and ponies are used, and in-struction is given by highly qualified professionals. Therapeutic riding helps physically handicapped, mentally retarded, learning-disabled, and emotionally disturbed children and adults adjust to and improve their handicapping conditions. It improves coordina-tion, posture, balance, strength, and muscle tone. It also fosters feelings of self-worth, self-confidence, and accomplishment.

Where would you fit into such a program? Probably as a volun-teer *walker* who would move alongside the horse or pony, helping the handicapped rider stay balanced, comfortable, at ease, and in control. You could do this independently with a participating sta-ble, or—more usually—as a member of a scout or 4-H group.

As part of your learning experience as a stable hand, you could perform similar duties with a riding instructor as he or she con-ducts beginners' lessons for regular students. It's a good beginning in learning to become a full-fledged riding instructor.

A riding instructor must be able to do two things well: to ride proficiently, and to convey that skill to others. The first attribute is self-evident; only the person capable of managing any horse in any situation from trail riding to show jumping with the confidence built through experience can do a proper job of teaching.

Communicating your skills calls for the ability to recognize and correct their lack in your students. Almost anyone can hang on to a horse. But achieving a proper seat and maintaining control through the use of hand and leg "aids" that a horse knows and will respond to are skills that must be taught. When beginning riders are instinctively good, the instructor must be able to recognize these skills and teach the rider how to improve on them. With most beginners, the instructor must be able to correct a host of mistakes and improve the student's performance by word and by example. With some students, this requires almost infinite patience.

The self-employed riding instructor charges from $45 and up for a riding lesson, depending on the number of students (the private lesson is more expensive) and the nature of the lesson. (For dressage or advanced jumping, the price may be as fancy as the hoofwork.)

HORSE TRAINER

Although there are certain procedures common to all forms of horse training, there are as many variations as there are needs for horses.

Among the traits shared by horse trainers are excellent health, an understanding of horse psychology and health, patience, gentleness, and the willingness to work long hours.

The sooner a trainer can work with a colt, the better. It's not unusual for a trainer to work for short periods with a foal, building a relationship through petting, soothing words, and gentle handling. The growing animal is taught in successive stages over a year or longer to accept a halter and be led on a short line without fear. The line is gradually lengthened and the colt is taught to start and stop on command, to go through its gaits (walk, trot, canter, perhaps pace, singlefoot or run, depending on breed and training). It is taught to stand still for grooming and to accept the confines of stableyard, barn, and ring. Later, it learns to accept bit, bridle, saddle, and harness cart, not always in this order. Eventually comes riding, sometimes by the familiar trainer, often by a co-trainer or assistant who rides while the trainer directs the proceedings, with—and later without—the long line. With consistency and kindness, the rider-trainer schools the young horse in the meaning of commands given by reins, knees, and heels. These aids are used to teach the horse when to change gait, slow down, turn, and stop, so that the response will be the same no matter who is riding.

"Bad dog! Bad dog!" We've often heard dogs scolded by their master or mistress.

"Bad horse!", on the other hand, is not a term used for that magnificent animal. But, indeed, horses *do* misbehave. It's a rare trainer who deals with a biting, stubborn horse. He or she will most likely choose to work with a well-behaved horse that will fly down the racetrack to a possible victory.

But Steve Grant—with the help of the John Lyon's training method—works with horses to discourage them from biting, bolting, and refusing a halter. His goal is to train horses without traumatizing them. He is strict but loving with his undisciplined animals. When they perform as he wishes, they are rewarded with hugs and pats.

Training uses the punishment-reward system, not with treats but with gentle words, pats, and relaxation in the saddle for a good performance; more stern speech, leg, and rein pressure will tell the horse, "Not so good—let's try that again." Stronger punishment is used sparingly and with great discretion.

That's basic training. Horses can be trained more specifically, depending on breed and purpose, and many trainers specialize. A hunter or show horse is taught to jump. A cowpony learns to change gait, stop, and turn instantly and accurately, and to react to the pull of the roped steer. A harness racer is taught to trot or pace at speed. Dressage and circus horses are patiently trained for their special work.

Horse trainers, specialized or not, learn their art by doing—usually starting as apprentices to established trainers. On a dude ranch or at a riding academy, you may begin as a groom and advance to trail ride leader and riding instructor. At racing stables and tracks, dedicated youngsters often begin as grooms, exercise riders, and hotwalkers who walk horses to exercise them and to cool them down after races or practice runs. This work develops the students' own riding talents.

Training, like instructing, is not known for its high pay. The "plus" side for you may be the chance to learn on the job, to work largely outdoors, to work seasonally or full-time, and—with luck and talent—to make a living based largely on your own increasing abilities rather than on formal education beyond high school—although this can often be extremely helpful.

The big money-makers among horse trainers are those able to recognize and develop equine and human talent for showmanship and particularly for racing. The racehorse trainer rarely owns the horses he or she trains, but trains them for the owners of stud farms and racing stables. The trainer's skills extend to selecting the best of the horses in his or her charge for specific events, and picking the right rider as well. In the case of show horses, the rider may be the owner, and the trainer may work with rider and mount as a team.

The more experienced racehorse trainers are often paid a percentage of their horses' winnings—usually 10 percent—and this may result in a very substantial income if you're dealing with big winners. More down-to-earth is a salary range of between $10,000 and $24,000 annually.

HORSE MASSAGER

Known more formally as *equine sports massage therapist,* these caregivers can bring relief to the race-weary, saddle-sore horse.

Horse massage is a recent development in equine care. Large-animal veterinarians and racetrack veterinarians are not sure that it makes a difference in the horse's well-being, but they are sure that the workout can't hurt. Some say their clients claim the horses really enjoy the deft and mindful care.

Massage therapist Theresa Wright-Williams of Colliersville, Tennessee, describes a racehorse named Murphy (valued at $50,000 to $100,000) whose right side was always stiff after racing. This was because racehorses only turn *left* when they race. No wonder they are sore on a side that never gets a proper workout! Wright-Williams uses massage techniques to ease Murphy's pain and increased his value.

Sandy Smith of Chalfont, Pennsylvania, took an equine massage course at Delaware Valley Community College, an agriculture and animal-oriented school. She is now an equine masseuse and works on horses ridden by inexperienced riders. A group of youngsters at summer camp can be a test of endurance for any horse. It's a weary animal that returns to the stable after a day of dug-in heels, and bouncing, hang-on-for-dear-life, middle schoolers.

If there is an agricultural and animal college near you, see if it has an equine massage course. The money you earn can be very good (in the case of thoroughbred racers) and the personal satisfaction rewarding.

LIFE ON A DUDE RANCH

Certainly nothing can better prepare a young man or woman for a life with that mysterious creature, the horse, than a season or two at a dude ranch. We're talking *rugged* here—but there's plenty of fun to be had during a summer spent outdoors, devoted to managing horses for ranch vacationers to ride. When you finish a season in one of these popular but highly athletic hostelries, there will be little you don't know about caring for a horse—or cleaning a stable!

Ranches may hire a young person for just one summer or for season after season. High school juniors and seniors and college students are those usually hired. They tend to return because they've learned the ropes (literally!) and they really enjoy the duties. (Hint: Apply early for summer work.)

You need not be a suburban or rural student to land a ranching job. Many wranglers and horse and mule pack guides come from eastern cities or midwestern towns.

For example, the Triangle X Dude Ranch consists of 1,500 acres for the dude ranch and 800 more for the horse ranch. The young ranch hands take care of more than 300 horses and mules used for riding and pack trips. Young women and men work together to ready these creatures for their duties. High school and college students will first perform simple equine chores, building toward the more intricate, physically demanding tasks of dealing with horses. Once they've mastered these skills, they become *wranglers.*

Wranglers corral the ranch horses, let them loose at night to graze on ranch lands, then feed and saddle them. On local rides—slow, intermediate, or at a gallop—two wranglers go along for the safety of the "dude" and the horse.

All wranglers and pack-trippers must learn first aid. They are also encouraged to know how to shoe a horse. Thus, life on the dude ranch caters to both the two-legged and four-legged creatures. But come evening, when the work is done the young workers will sing or play guitars under a star-filled sky. It's the real thing—not a "horse opera" (slang for a western movie).

Most dude ranch workers will put in one, two, or three summers. By then, they are ready to go into horse training, breeding, and racing if these are their animal care career goals. What more memorable way could there possibly be to start an equine career than on a dude ranch?

PROFESSIONAL RIDERS

Anyone who primarily earns a living by riding horses is technically a professional rider. But the term also applies to Grand Prix horse show contestants and is usually reserved for harness racing drivers and flat racing jockeys. They are professionals inasmuch as they are paid in proportion to their skills and victories versus defeats, just as other professional athletes are. Being a Grand Prix rider, harness driver, or jockey generally isn't something a "horse person" starts off being; rather, it is something they eventually may become after months or years of long hours spent in hard, time-consuming work with horses.

Talent and luck have a lot to do with whether or not you as an exerciser or apprentice trainer ever get a shot at professional riding. Size and weight aren't too important in Grand Prix racing, competitive dressage, circus work, or even in harness racing, but to the would-be thoroughbred jockey, less is more. A normal weight without constant dieting of 105 to 112 pounds is essential; the less weight a race horse carries, the better.

Alison Kramer of New Jersey fell in love with horses at age eleven when she learned to ride at an equestrian school. After graduating from high school, Alison worked with show horses and later had a job training yearlings.

Later, Alison worked as an exerciser at racetracks in New Jersey, New York, and Florida, "but I always wanted to be a jockey," she says.

Finally, she was given her chance. Trainer Henry Carroll let her race "Quick Hitch" at Monmouth (NJ) Race Course. Although she finished sixth in a ten-horse race, "it was a great experience."

For every Steve Cauthen—the first jockey to earn $6,000,000 for riding 488 winners in one year—there are hundreds who work under contract to racing stable owners for a salary-plus-bonus for wins, or who freelance, picking up "rides" at the request of trainers who match them with suitable horses. Travel expenses and costly riding gear are usually the jockey's responsibility, and their costs can cut severely into earnings—jockeys must travel to race "meetings" throughout the country. High incomes are not unusual for jockeys with good reputations—but not celebrity status. Racing is held only when, and where, it is warm but not hot. In this seasonal work, there may be several "dry" months a year—and jockeying is definitely an early-retirement career. Retired jockeys often work in other areas of racing. One English steeplechaser, Dick Francis, is a highly successful mystery novel writer! The horse racing world provides the setting for his plots.

OTHER TRACK CAREERS AND BLACKSMITHING

There are careers on racetracks for experienced people who work with horses but don't necessarily ride them. During a meeting, racetracks will employ racing secretaries, stewards, judges, veterinarians, specialists who tattoo horses' lips to identify them, and identifiers who verify the horses' identities against their tattoos and their registration papers before they can race.

Then, there is the blacksmith, often called a smith, farrier, or horseshoer. Only the most skilled may be licensed to work at racetracks, but whether at the track or the horse farm, the job is equally demanding.

We'll bet there's at least one blacksmith whose truck reads "We Make Horse Calls," for indeed they do. The "village smithy" no longer stands "under the spreading chestnut tree" but rolls instead, from stud farm to racetrack to riding academy. Although there are some women farriers, Longfellow's poetic line, "The smith a mighty man is he" generally holds true, for horseshoeing calls for a strong back, legs, and arms. It's work that should be started early in life, according to professionals.

There is a difference, though. Today's blacksmith is more equine podiatrist than ironworker. In fact, with most racehorses, the shoe of choice is lightweight aluminum. In many cases, the inbreeding that has been used to develop racehorses with great speed may also have created the hoof problems that the blacksmith must recognize and correct. This is done by tailoring the fit of the shoe. Although the farrier's experience helps determine the correction that must be made, the desired result is often a matter of trying and trying again until the racehorse's speed, gait, and comfort are right.

The blacksmith's day starts early—especially at racetracks. Each previous day's thrown shoes or other problems must be solved before the horses' morning workouts. The rest of the day at the races is taken up with routine shoe changes and consulting with trainers and jockeys on problems that arise.

Racetrack work usually involves testing and licensing, but whether or not a farrier works at the track, he or she may take smithing courses in vo-tech high school as career preparation and definitely should serve an apprenticeship with a skilled smith. A blacksmith must, of course, be able to handle horses, often when they are not on their best behavior.

Need for tailoring and special shoes extends to show and pleasure horses, too.

In addition to a sturdy pickup truck, 4 X 4, or van, today's blacksmith needs to invest in the equipment of the craft: powered grinder, drill press, forge, anvil, gas torches, and finishing tools (knives, rasps, etc.). This is at least a several-thousand-dollar investment.

An experienced blacksmith may be able to shoe from five to ten horses a day, depending on the travel involved. The money is such that a capable blacksmith with a following can enjoy a good living plus a fair degree of independence.

EDUCATION

The education in high school and beyond described in the horse breeder profile would be excellent training for most horse careers, as a supplement to learning-by-doing. There are a small but growing number of colleges and junior colleges that offer courses related to horsemanship. Some schools of equitation offer certificates of proficiency.

Harcum Junior College in Bryn Mawr, Pennsylvania, is close to the world-famous Devon Horse Show grounds; Chesterland, the site of national horse trials; and the Radnor Hunt Club. Over the past ten years, Harcum has established itself in the field of animal health care by offering majors in many animal care areas. The school has recently added an associate degree program in equine studies. Among the electives are equine breeding, therapeutic riding, equine business management, and teaching equitation. To prepare for these careers, students at Harcum take courses in animal biology, equine health and disease, lameness, equitation theory, equitation instruction, organization of events, stable management, and equine business management.

The Harcum program has equivalent programs in other parts of the country. School counselors, librarians, and veterinary technical schools should be able to direct you to this field that offers everything: the bountiful outdoors, mental and physical challenges, and the constant company of one of nature's most beautiful creatures, the horse.

VETERINARY MEDICAL SCHOOLS

U.S. SCHOOLS

Alabama

Auburn University
  Office for Academic Affairs
  College of Veterinary Medicine
  217 Goodwin Student Center
  Auburn University, AL 36849-5536
  www.vetmed.auburn.edu

Tuskegee University
  School of Veterinary Medicine
  Tuskegee, AL 36088

California

University of California
  Office of the Dean-Student Programs
  School of Veterinary Medicine
  One Shields Avenue
  Davis, CA 95616
  www.ucdavis.edu

Colorado

Colorado State University
  Office of the Dean
  College of Veterinary Medicine and Biomedical Sciences
  Fort Collins, CO 80523-1601
  www.cvmbs.colostate.edu

Florida

University of Florida
  Office for Students and Instruction
  College of Veterinary Medicine
  P. O. Box 100125
  Gainesville, FL 32610-0125
  www.vetmed.ufl.edu

Georgia

University of Georgia
  Office for Academic Affairs
  College of Veterinary Medicine
  Athens, GA 30602-7372
  www.vet.uga.edu

Illinois

University of Illinois at Urbana-Champaign
  Office of Academic and Student Affairs
  College of Veterinary Medicine
  22716 Veterinary Medicine Basic Sciences Building
  2001 South Lincoln Avenue
  Urbana, IL 61802
  www.cvm.uiuc.edu

Indiana

Purdue University
  Student Services Office
  School of Veterinary Medicine
  1240 Lynn Hall
  West Lafayette, IN 47907-1240
  www.vet.purdue.edu

Iowa

Iowa State University
  Office of Admissions
  Room 100, Alumni Hall
  Ames, IA 50011
  www.vetmed.iastate.edu

Kansas

Kansas State University
  Office of the Assistant Dean
  College of Veterinary Medicine
  102A Trotter Hall
  1700 Denison Avenue
  Manhattan, KS 66506-5601
  www.vet.ksu.edu

Louisiana

Louisiana State University
  Office of Veterinary Student Affairs
  School of Veterinary Medicine
  Baton Rouge, LA 70803
  www.vetmed.lsu.edu

Massachusetts

Tufts University
  Office of Admissions
  School of Veterinary Medicine
  200 Westboro Road
  North Grafton, MA 01536
  www.tufts.edu/vet/

Michigan

Michigan State University
  Admissions Office
  College of Veterinary Medicine
  A-126 East Fee Hall
  East Lansing, MI 48824-1316
  www.cvm.msu.edu

Minnesota

University of Minnesota
  Office of Student Affairs and Admissions
  College of Veterinary Medicine
  460 Veterinary Teaching Hospital
  1365 Gortner Avenue
  St. Paul, MN 55108
  www.cvm.umn.edu

Mississippi

Mississippi State University
  Office of Student Affairs
  College of Veterinary Medicine
  P. O. Box 9825
  Mississippi State, MS 39762
  www.cvm.msstate.edu

Missouri

University of Missouri-Columbia
    Office of Academic Affairs
    College of Veterinary Medicine
    W203 Veterinary Medicine Building
    Columbia, MO 65211
    www.missouri.edu

New York

Cornell University
    Office of D.V.M. Admissions
    College of Veterinary Medicine
    S1-006 Schurman Hall
    Ithaca, NY 14853-6401
    www.vet.cornell.edu

North Carolina

North Carolina State University
    Office of Student Services
    College of Veterinary Medicine
    4700 Hillsborough Street
    Raleigh, NC 27606
    www.cvm.ncsu.edu

Ohio

The Ohio State University
    Chairperson, Admissions Committee
    College of Veterinary Medicine
    0004 Veterinary Hospital
    601 Tharp Street
    Columbus, OH 43210-1089
    www.vet.ohio-state.edu/docs/

Oklahoma

Oklahoma State University
  Admissions Office
  College of Veterinary Medicine
  Stillwater, OK 74078-2003
  www.okstate.edu

Oregon

Oregon State University
  Office of the Dean
  College of Veterinary Medicine
  200 Magruder Hall
  Corvallis, OR 97331-4801
  www.vet.orst.edu

Pennsylvania

University of Pennsylvania
  Admissions Office
  School of Veterinary Medicine
  3800 Spruce Street
  Philadelphia, PA 19104-6044
  www.vet.upenn.edu

Tennessee

University of Tennessee
  Office of the Associate Dean
  College of Veterinary Medicine
  P.O. Box 1071
  Knoxville, TN 37901-1071
  www.vet.utk.edu

Texas

Texas A & M University
  Office of the Dean
  College of Veterinary Medicine
  College Station, TX 77843-4461
  www.cvm.tamu.edu

Virginia

Virginia Polytechnic Institute and State University
  Admissions Coordinator
  Virginia-Maryland Regional College of Veterinary Medicine
  Blacksburg, VA 24061
  www.vetmed.vt.edu

Washington

Washington State University
  Office of Student Services
  College of Veterinary Medicine
  Pullman, WA 99164-7012

Wisconsin

University of Wisconsin-Madison
  Office of Academic Affairs
  School of Veterinary Medicine
  2015 Linden Drive West
  Madison, WI 53706-1102
  www.vetmed.wisc.edu.oaa/oaa.html

CANADIAN SCHOOLS

Montreal

Université de Montreal
  Service des Admissions
  C.P. 6205
  Succursale Centre-Ville
  Montreal, Quebec H3C 3T5
  Canada
  www.medvet.umontreal.ca

Ontario

University of Guelph
  Admissions, Office of the Registrar
  University Centre, Level 3
  Guelph, Ontario N1G 2W1
  Canada
  or
  Assistant Dean for Student Affairs
  Ontario Veterinary College
  www.ovc-uoguelph.ca

Prince Edward Island

University of Prince Edward Island
  Registrar's Office
  Atlantic Veterinary College
  550 University Avenue
  Charlottetown, Prince Edward Island C1A 4P3
  Canada
  www.upei.ca/~regoff/

Saskatchewan

University of Saskatchewan
    Admissions Office
    Western College of Veterinary Medicine
    52 Campus Drive
    Saskatoon, Saskatchewan S7N 5B4
    Canada
    www.usask.ca/wcvm

BIBLIOGRAPHY

Beck, Alan, and Aaron Katcher. *Between Pets and People: The Importance of Animal Companionship.* West Lafayette, IN: University of Purdue Press, 1996.

Ellison, Joan Jarvis. *Shepherdess, Notes from the Field.* West Lafayette, IN: University of Purdue Press, 1995. (A former biophysical science major, this lady retired to Minnesota to raise her children and a flock of sheep. It's a heartwarming story.)

Heath, Sebastian. *Rescuing Rover: A First Aid and Disaster Guide for Dog Owners.* West Lafayette, IN: University of Purdue Press, 2000.

Veterinary Medical School Admissions Requirements for the United States and Canada. Compiled by the Association of American Veterinary Medical Colleges. West Lafayette, IN: University of Purdue Press, 1999.